I DON'T LIKE YOU

YOU

∙∙

Kamala Davis

Contents

Her next door neighbor, which she hates, now has to drive her to school and back every day. He's cocky, and she has an attitude, which he really doesn't like.

I m finally a junior in high school. I've always wanted to be a junior, only one grade above me, but not too many people to intimidate me. In fact nowadays people usually find me to be the intimidating one.

Black and purple hair, falling just below my shoulders. Eyeliner, docs, and my leather jacket. Im so hot.

I walk out of my room to eat breakfast, seeing my next door neighbour sitting at the breakfast bar. I love her. She's basically like a second mom to me.

I stop dead in my tracks though when I see her asshole son Ryan. My breath hitches. "Good morning darling," my mom says from the kitchen.

I smile and give her a hug, avoiding eye contact with Ryan the whole time I make my cereal, though I could feel his heavy stare.

"So Alice, my dear boy here has agreed to give you a ride to school this year since-"

"What?"

My mom laughs awkwardly, she knows I don't like him, why is she allowing this? I thought she was giving me rides this year. I put my cereal bowl down, still standing there.

"That's - great. I mean thanks." I look towards him, and meet his gaze. Which is hard and pissed off.

"Let's go we'll be late." I look towards my mom, a last desperate plea, but hear, "todayyy." God.

I get in the car, attempting to take the back seat to sit as far from him as possible.

He turns around and says, "Im not a fucking uber driver, get your ass up here."

Even though we've been neighbours, I've never really gotten along with him. He smokes, and was always in the more popular group. Black hair, and a nice body he fits right in.

I roll my eyes and move up, sitting uncomfortably close to him in his small lancer. "Don't roll your eyes at me you ungrateful brat, if it weren't for me you'd have to walk."

"Excuse me?" I scoff at his arrogance, rolling my eyes again and I see his fingers tighten on the gear shift.

When we get to school we each go our separate ways, and I only have to see him second period during ligature. Don't know why he's taking this class, don't know if he's ever even held a book.

During lunch I see my best friend Katie. I love her to death. She's hippy in the best way possible, and loves nature and crystals and plants. Her vibes make everyone smile, and pretty much everyone likes her.

I told her about what happened this morning and she totally agrees that he's a stupid ass.

After the silent ride home, I immediately call my mom. "Hey mom!"

"Hey sweaty how was school?"

"Ya um, so why can't you drive me to school anymore? I thought that like you know you would drive me and I'd walk home with Katie this year?"

"Oh, well I thought you'd be happy to have a drive both ways, and his mom was just so excited to be able to help out. And with your brother in the hospital I thought I could see him instead- but you know if you want me to drive you I still can."

"No, no mom I was just wondering. I'll see you later, say hi to Ben for me." I say with a smile.

———————

I wake up the next day, to a slam. I jolt awake, pulling the covers over my sports bra. I look to the door and find Ryan standing there.

"What the fuck are you doing here!!"

"Watch your self. Your late. It's 8." My eyes widen as I turn to look at the clock.

"Shit I forgot to set my alarm. Fuck." I jump outta bed, and run to my dresser completely forgetting Ryans standing there, while Im in a sports bra and underwear. "Shit, get out!" I say again.

His mouth slowly pulls up into a smirk, and he slides out the door arms held up.

When I get downstairs he's back to his usual self.

2

Ryan waking me up in the morning has become sort of routine. He'll come in, make some snarky comment, as I shoo him out the door. At least now I sleep in clothes.

Today was no different. Except he seemed super pissed off. He came right up to my bed today, and yanked me out of it by my arm. "Hey!"

"Hurry up I have to be there early today."

"Why?"

He steps up to me, and looks down from his tall frame. "I said I have to be there. That's it. Fuck, where are your fucking clothes." My cheeks turn bright red, my memory flashes back to the first time he came in here.

"It was hot-last night." His eyes trail down my body.

"Buy a fan." And he walks out. For some reason my heart has gotten faster, and I swallow.

When I get downstairs there's a note on the counter that says, "your walking," in messy writing. Well this is what I get for putting eyeliner on today.

I'm talking to Katie at school, and she's telling me about some guy she's talking to. Not any guy, some guy from Ryans group of dicks. "Katie you know he's a player."

"Well ya, but he's so cute. And of course if I become a thing with him, we could get invited to parties!!"

"Haha right. That actually true," I look across the hall and see Ryan standing with his friends. Why are all the hot ones the shit ones.

"I think.....We actually....tonight can I pleaseee come over so you can help me pick out an outfit?"

"Sorry what?" I zoned out. Shit.

"I said I think it's a great idea. We actually have a date tonight so can I pleaseee come over so you can help me pick out an outfit?

"Oh ya of course. I'll just have to ask the asshole if he won't mind driving you. He ditched me this morning for god knows what."

"Aw. Alright we'll I'll see you at lunch, let me know."

"Yup."

I walk over to Ryan, who's now alone thankfully, and he slams his locker shut. "What do you want."

"Hi to you too. So you mind if Katie gets a ride with me to my house?"

He sighs really heavy. "No".

"Please."

He thinks pretend hard for a minute. "No." He starts walking.

"Please." He sighs heavy again.

"Fine, but you'll owe me one." I smile and walk away happily towards my class.

Later, me and Katie run upstairs, and she jumps onto my bed. "Soooo, I may have lied a little bit."

"Mmk, what do you mean?"

"So remember how I told you that if I went on this date with him he'd invite us to parties?"

"Yes, and?"

"And so we're going to a party tonight!"

"Your kidding?" Me and Katie love to party. Us+drinking is lots of fun. We do lots of dancing and usually kiss plenty of boys. Or girls if she feels like it.

For the next 2 hours we tried on outfits, and did our hair and makeup. I went for a short red dress, while she went with a flowery sun dress. We both looked hot.

Now we just needed a ride. The part I dreaded most. If only I had a car.

The phone starts to ring, and on the second ring he picks up. "Heeeey." I pause. No response. "So are you going to that party tonight by any chance?"

"No. I'm not your fucking uber Alice." I sigh.

"I'll owe you double! I swear." I could practically hear his teeth gridding. But he does love to have something on me.

"Fine." He says lowly. "But your paying me back tonight."

"Fine, whatever." I smile and give Katie a thumbs up.

We leave out the door, and Ryan is there waiting for us. I swear I see his eyes trailing up and down my body. "You look like a stripper," he says flatly. Of course. When I reach for the back door he says, "front." Ugh. He's such an ass.

Katie and I talk almost the whole ride there, until he turns the rock station all the way up making it impossible.

I turn it back down, and he gives me a side glance. He turns it back up, daring me to turn it back down.

I almost do, until we pull into a driveway. Finally. We walk into the house, and me and Katie immediately are taking a few shots and heading to the dance floor. She ditches me after about an hour though, probably to go make out with Kris. I still don't like him even if he got us into this party. I'm left to dance alone, not that I minded.

I'm already tipsy, when I feel hands taking my waist.

Before I can turn around I hear a whisper in my ear, "time for that favour love."

"Love?"

"Kiss me," he spins me around, and before I can blink his lips are on mine. They move fast, and all I can do is give in. I can feel his smirk. His lips move down to my neck and it finally licks it when I'm about to moan that we are in a room full of people.

"Hey! What the hell!"

"Shh." He leans down to my face. "Look behind you."

I turn around a bit and see a girl standing there, looking absolutely shocked. "Um-"

"Need something Sofia? If not run along Im busy."

I stand there, as I watch her walking away, "seriously?" I ask. "Was there no other way to tell her no?"

He shrugs and smirks. "More fun seeing you all flustered." He laughs, "and I mean you owed me one."

I stomp away frustrated. How dare he? Kiss me like that in front of all of these people?! He grabs my arm and yanks me back. "Hey. I still have one more favour."

"And what is it that you want?" I say bitchily.

"First off, cut it out."

I scoff, and attempt to walk away, this time he lets me get as far as the hallway when he slams me into the wall.

3

He slams me into the wall, as people are walking by. "I've just about had it with your fucking attitude these past few days. I said you fucking owe me one."

"Who the hell do you think you are, shut up and let me go."

"Listen, the only reason why I'm nice to you is because your my best friends sister. And he just happens to be injured, so I agreed to look out for you. But if your going to keep up with this fucking bitchy-"

"Just shut up already will you? I'm sorry you feel obligated you prick, I'll be walking from now on. And don't worry about driving me home, I'll walk home tonight too."

For some reason this really pisses him off. He grabs my wrist firmly and pulls me away, into a study. "You're not walking anywhere looking like that," he whispers under his breath as he drags me away, I barley caught it.

Once we're in the study I wiggle out of his grasp, but he grabs my wrists and pushes me into the wall. I could tell he was a little bit drunk.

"What are you doing!"

He trails his eyes down my body, "whys your breathing so harsh Alice?" One hand takes both my wrists above my head, and the other trails down my face to lightly brush my neck.

"I-um" I swallow and take a breath. "What's the favour you needed?"

"I need you to tell me something," his hand slowly stretches, across my neck.

"Mm o-kay." My breathing is extremely fast now, and his knee slides between my legs which makes it somehow speed up even more. I look down at my feet.

Slowly he says, "Why did you say no to me in 9th grade?" His hand is now fully wrapped around my neck, and a little whimper comes out of me as his grip begins to tighten. He pushes my head back up to look at him.

"I- well- you were a year older, and you um," I struggle to get the words out, hating how intimidated I feel right now. My legs though, try to clench together before remembering his leg between them.

"I-um," he smirks mocking me, pushing his leg up higher, which now rubs against me.

My brows knot together, and I'm starting to get annoyed. "You were ugly." I smile innocently. His grips tighter. "And you were an asshole." Tighter. "And I wanted someone more... interesting." I barley get the last words out, my face flushed red. "Stop."

His grip lessens slightly, his nostrils flaring. "I'm going to fucking end you."

"Aw, poor boy can't handle rejection?" Fuck I should not taunt him right now. But I can't control the way my body reacts to him being pissed off. The excitement running through me.

I struggle under him, and he smirks again thinking of something. " 'You Were ugly?' " He repeats. I stop and stare at him, then drop my gaze. "And what about now?" He pushes my head up once more, forcing eye contact. "Am I stillboring?" His grip tightens again. No you're fucking hot.

"Y-yes. Ugly- and so so boring." His jaw clenches and he finally lets me go, standing over me while I crouch over to catch my breath.

His face looks red with anger, but he calmly says, "Get the fuck out. I'll call you and Katie an uber home." Then he takes off his leather jacket and throws it over me. "And your never wearing that dress again."

4

I wake up beside Katie in my bed, and frown as all the memories from last night hit me. Thank god it's a saturday, and I don't have to see his stupid face. I mean who the hell does he think he is?

I can't help feeling turned on though by his hand pressing my wrists to the wall. Or his hand around my...

"Morning," I say to Katie cutting my thoughts short. She had way more to drink last night than I had, and I found her passed out beside Kris in some random guest bedroom. Luckily they were both moderately clothed.

She whines and rolls over, shoving her face into the pillow.

"Come on, wake up dumbass, we have to go eat something."

"Ughhh, give me five more minutes, christ."

I laugh and look at the clock. It's already 1pm. I get up, shoving the clothes on my floor away and walk to my bathroom. I'm still wearing my makeup from last night, but disregarded the dress. I throw on a big tshirt, and some tight shorts.

I clean my self up, and shower, by the time Katie wakes up and stumbles her way into the bathroom.

My parents are gone at the hospital with my brother, so as usual it's just me making some pancakes for the two of us.

I assume Katie told her mom she'd be here for the night, but just in case I texted her.

I look out the kitchen window, and see Ryan in the front yard mowing the lawn. Shirtless. He looks so hot... I mean gross. And sweaty.

Fuck me.

Katie walks down and we eat our pancakes. I eat mine with jam, while she eats hers with more maple syrup than pancake.

I hear a knock at the door, and head over to see who it is.

"Who is it?" Katie yells from the kitchen.

"No one."

I turn around and walk back to the kitchen to keep eating.

That's when the front door opens, and in he walks. When the hell did he get a key? I guess I never questioned how he comes in every morning to wake me up even when my parents aren't home.

He walks towards us, and I remind myself not to stare. "Your mom asked for me to mow your lawn, but I'll need your lawn mower."

"Why not use yours?"

"Yours is better, and since you have a bigger lawn..." he shrugged. "Can you open the shed or not?" He says impatiently, but unlike me has no problem making eye contact the entire time.

"Um ya," I mumble. I don't want to be alone with him. Even if just for a few seconds.

Katie looks between us, silently asking if she missed something.

I walk outside, slipping on sandals. I open the shed and walk inside to show him where it is.

But before I can get too far he grabs my hips and pushes me against the work bench, leaning into my neck. I nearly stop breathing, and go totally still.

"Your going to regret what you said last night. Don't think I forgot." His naked torso leans against mine and I shut my eyes trying not to stare.

"I don't know what your talking about," I say quietly. He has no issues with my current state, and stares right down my top.

"And I want my jacket back at school Monday." His thumb traces a line on my hip, absent mindedly, as if it was the most casual thing in the world.

"Okay.." My heart beat is running a mile per minute.

He takes one last look at me before stepping back, and walking towards the lawn mower. I take that as my que to leave. I'm in the door he says, "Oh, and Alice?"

"Ya?"

"My eyes are up here." I look up and flush red, speed walking out of the shed. I can hear him chuckling behind me. Fucking- arrogant-prick-

As I walk back into the house, Katie is already waiting for me at the door.

"So wanna tell me what all that tension was about?"

"It's nothing."

She crosses her arms. "Did something happen at the party?"

"Sort of..." I trail off, and look behind me out the window when I hear the lawn mower starting up.

"You slept with him didn't you!!"

"What?! No! God no."

She sighed, "so what happened."

"Well..."

So I told her bits of what happened. I left out the choking, and the pinning against the wall parts, but told her the basics of the conversation. And how he kissed me while we danced.

"Damn. You should totally fuck him. I mean I would've, if I didn't know that you have a crush on him."

"I do not!!"

"Uh-huh. Your blushing. And either way, he's totally hot."

"Whatever."

My alarm went off at 7:30 this morning, and I aggressively hit the snooze button. Regrettably though I get up out of bed, not expecting Ryan to come in this morning.

However. To my suprise, and his that I'm awake, he walks in ready to go as always. I hate morning people.

He smirks crossing his arms, leaning against the dresser and says, "wow someone's up for once."

"Shut up."

His eyes trail me as I walk to the same dresser to get out black jeans and a black t-shirt.

"Well, I'm up. Get out."

"Do You ever wear any other colour?"

"Black matches everything. And you do the same." He looks away towards my closet, where the red dress is still on the floor.

"Where's my jacket?"

"I'll get it to you, but right now I have to get ready, so leave."

"Not leaving until you give it back."

"It's downstairs you ass, go get it yourself."

He squints his eyes at me, and walks downstairs. I get undressed, putting on my bra, when he walks back in.

"I can't find it."

"Oh my god! Give me a minute!" I struggle to clasp my bra up.

He sighs and walks over, smacking my hands away.

"I don't need your help."

"Mhm. I know you don't. Give me my jacket or I won't leave."

"Fine suite yourself." I get dressed right in front of him, shoving it in his face that I'm unbothered. Even if I totally am. I could feel his stare from a mile away. I finish getting dressed while he watches. I swear I see his cheeks pink.

"Done?"

I walk downstairs ignoring him, and grab his beloved jacket out of the closet. "Happy?" I throw it at him, hard.

My mind still can't get him shirtless and against me out of my head. And it's pissing me off.

The school the day goes on as normal, except during second period when he sits down beside me instead of his usual seat at the back. "What book are you reading?" He asks.

I look at him as if he grew two heads. Did he just ask a genuine question? Not mocking or anything?

"Um, Shatter Me. It's about-"

"Right, yeah. I actually don't care." Of course. What was I thinking. "I need you to come over tonight and help me with something."

"So what you'll only talk to me to mock me or when you need something from me?"

"As if you do any different?" True.

"Fine. Help you with what. And you'll owe me one." He smirks at my comment.

"Of course. You'll see."

I go back to reading my book, when he snatches it out of my hands. "So what's it about again?"

"Hey! Give it back!"

I'm on the third I think book of the series- in other words this book has a few... scenes in it?

"Why? Is this one of those books with smut in it or something?" My cheeks heat up, and and he looks at me smiling. "You know I think I might borrow this."

I cross my arms and sit back in my seat. I'll take it back on the way home.

In the caf, Im sitting with Katie when a cute guy walks up to us. His names Jake I think?

"Hey," he smiles at me.

"Hi, Jake is it?"

"Ya. So - I was wondering if maybe you wanted to go out tonight, there's this place it has really good smoothies?"

"Ya! Sure I'd love to."

"Great here's my number, say around 4?" He writes it down on a napkin and as soon as he leaves Katie quietly shrieks in my ear.

Im actually a bit excited. I've seen him around, but I didn't know he knew me. He's cute, in like a, I'd buy you a puppy kinda way.

Later when Im walking to class, my arm gets pulled hard, and I'm in a empty classroom. My back is flesh against a hard surface, and when his arm wraps around my neck I freeze knowing exactly who it is. My arms shoot up to grab his, but it's no use. One is wrapped around my waist while the other is around my neck.

"I heard you had a date later?" Ryan says.

"Ya and?" His grip grows tighter.

"I thought I told you your with me tonight?" He shoves me away from him, and I feel much clearer headed.

"Well I made better plans."

"Too bad you have no way of getting there."

"Actually, he has a car. Said he'll pick me up."

His teeth grit together. "Fine. If I'm done with you by then, you can go."

"Who the fuck do you think you are telling me who I can, and cannot see?"

"Listen to me very carefully." He steps closer, and I move back against a desk suddenly feeling very small. His hands lean on the desk on either side of me. "You will come to my house tonight. Whether you like it or not. And you'll text him that your not sure if you'll be able to make it but you'll call ahead. Understand?"

I'm about to argue when the bell rings, and he leaves me standing there in a furry.

While we're driving I again ask for my book back, and even told him that it's not the first book, but he just says that he'll borrow the first two as well.

When we pull into his driveway, his mom greats me with a hug as I walk into the door. She says that dinner will be ready for 5 and Im welcome to stay as long as I want. How is this even her son?

We walk upstairs to his room, and it's really nice. I've never actually been in here before, just peered inside.

It's all black and dark greys, a few fake plants (Im guessing his mom added those, she loves greenery)

"So what did you need help with?" I want to get out of here as fast as possible.

"I want a mural on my wall, and you paint don't you?" Oh. Well that was unexpected.

"I mean ya, sometimes, but not really walls."

"You have things painted all over your walls though."

"I mean ya but I mean Ive never painted something for someone else. Why do you want a mural aren't you moving out in like a year?"

"I don't know, I think it'd be cool. And my mom says I need more colour in here. Plus, it would mean having you here more and not in your house all alone... My mom doesn't like that." Right... his mom doesn't.

"Okay well I guess. You'll owe me one though. And your buying the paint yourself Im not using mine.

"Fine."

"So what do you want on it?"

"I don't know maybe some sort of cityscape thing. I still have to live in here. I don't want some sort of floral shit." I have roses on my walls. Dying ones but still, ouch.

"Okay well I'll start a design on it tonight. Bye." I walk towards the door, but he slams it shut in my face his hand leaning over me.

"No. You'll start it now."

"You realize this is a favour right? I don't have to do this. I have a date to get ready for." At that his face contracts into a ugly frown.

"Right. Well I need help with the ligature assignment."

"You have the highest grade in the class," he looks at me for an explanation, "that teacher likes me." I shrug.

He sighs annoyingly, "well Im out of ideas. Your just not going. That's it."

"Great good for you. But I'm leaving"-

"Just shut the fuck up," he shoves me onto the bed, then throws me a sketch book from his desk as well as a pencil.

I look at him annoyed. "Draw a design and you can go. My mom will want to see it."

I sigh. Always using his mom. Can't he just say he doesn't want me going? Is he jealous!?

"Don't tell me your jealous of Jake?" I laugh a little.

He says nothing.

"Oh my god! You are! Ha!"

He comes up to the bed then, and pins my arms above my head. Seems he really likes this position...

He likes to be over me, overpowering me in anyway possible. Almost-dominate me.

Immediately my breathing gets faster at his proximity, and my skin begins to tingle.

"And what if I am? Would you consider not going?"

I think for a minute. "Maybe if you begged me to stay." I smirk like he so often does.

"Your such a fucking brat." His grip is unbreakable, even as I struggle to get out.

"I'm not a child." He huffs a laugh.

"You wouldn't get the term." I look at him confused. "You know if you want to leave now why not just go?" He smiles.

I look his stupid arrogant face. "Right thanks," and his grip tightens just to prove a point

His hands shift, and one trails down my body. "I could make you want to stay so easily."

His hand reaches my stomach and my heart stops, his thumb pressing in.

That's when I hear his mom calling us for dinner. Shit is it 5 already??? I don't even realize he stoped holding me down a few seconds ago.

6

I jump up, and he lets me, as I run to check my phone. I quickly dial his number, and it's ringing as I feel Ryan behind my back.

"Guess you can't make it to your date, huh?" His arms wrap around me possessively. I try to shove him away but he won't move.

"Hey Jake it's Alice!"

"Oh hey, I though you forgot. I could've sworn I said 4?" God he's so nice I feel so bad.

"No I"- Ryans hand moves to my lower stomach, and I feel his lips on my neck. "Um I just got caught up with homework." I try smacking his head away, but he won't stop.

"Right well, the place is open till 7, so if you still wanna go I can pick you up now?"

Ryan grabs my chin, pulling it to the side and starts to suck on my neck. "Fuck stop that," I whisper.

"Sorry what? I think it cut out."

"Oh- no ya that would be great. I'll see you in like 30?"

"Ya"-

"K! Bye!" I hang up the phone and turn towards Ryan, shoving him back into the bed. "What the fuck is wrong with you??"

He sits there smirking while I look on my phone camera to see a huge hickie, right where my neck meets my shoulder.

"Have fun on your date," he says flatly, but with a little smile. He walks out of the room, and I storm back home. Now I have to figure out how to hide this thing in 20 minutes! I hate him!!

I search up heaps of youtube videos but no amount of concealer can cover it. Even a whisk didn't work.

"Ugh!"

I call Jake to cancel. There's no point in going with this on my neck. I'm going to fucking kill that man. Im honestly not as disappointed as I thought I'd be though. Jake is really nice- but that's the thing he's, just soo nice. Too nice?

Later his mom comes over with left overs from their dinner, and I gratefully take them up to my room.

I Facetime Katie for a bit, and tell her about the weird mural thing. She suggested I ask his mom about it, to see if it's actually legit.

The next afternoon after school I find my mom and dad downstairs in the kitchen. They're talking about possibly renting out an apartment closer to the hospital, so they have a closer living situation with my brother.

He got in a car accident, and might be paralyzed, but they're still working it out. He can wiggle his toes so it's possible that with lots of physical therapy he'll eventually be able to walk again.

But it also means lots of doctors appointments. And lots of treatment. Which means lots of time with him.

When Ryan walks in with his mom, he looks me up and down, and tells me to come upstairs for a sec.

I turn the corner and he pulls my shirt over my head. "You're not wearing this."

"What did you just say to me?" It was a red crop top, with some lace along the top. I was about to go out with Katie to do some shopping.

He pulls out a oversized tshirt from my drawers and throws it at me.

"This is literally a pyjama shirt." I say.

"You want to get to the mall or not?" Why did he have to offer to drive us?! Apparently he 'needs stuff from there anyway.' As if. He's just a possessive idiot.

"You can't tell me what to wear."

"I can and I will." He smirks. "Or do I need to get you submissive for me. Then will you listen?"

"What?-" His hand wraps around my throat, and he pushes me into the wall, his other hand resting by my head.

I gasp, and he says, "now will you listen?" I gulp.

"I-I'll wear whatever I want to wear." His hand trails down my side, reaching my hip.

Then he leans in and says, "did I tell you you could cover up my hickie?" He stares down, and I become very aware that I'm in just a bra.

"Fine I'll wear the damned shirt. And I obviously had to cover it up for school you dumbass."

"How about you try again with less attitude."

Oh he's just itching for a knee up his ass.

"Fuck off." He takes a deep breath.

"Cancel your plans," he says now very seriously.

"What?"

"What the fuck did I tell you about your fucking attitude?"

"But"-

"Cancel, your fucking plans. And do me a favour, keep quiet, wouldn't want anyone downstairs to hear you." He shuts the door with his foot, and pushes me to the bed, his hand still around my neck.

"What do you mean..?" I let out an involuntary moan, as he drags a finger along my clit.

"Shh, what did I tell you about being quiet?" I whimper as his hand slips under my black skirt, and he hands me my phone, causing him to release the tight grasp he had on my neck. I attempt to get up, but he forces my shoulder back down, and rubs hard again. I'm so turned on right now I practically see stars. "Call her. Now." I can hear the wetness as he moves my underwear aside.

I moan again as he circles my clit. "St-stop then," I choke out.

"Call. Her," his hand wraps around my throat again, "Now."

I fumble with the phone as I call her. She picks up on the third ring. "Hey-I um can't go to the mall anymore." I squirm under him trying to move away.

"Oh- how come is everything okay?" I shut my eyes, trying my hardest to keep quiet.

"Why are you so wet Alice?" He hums into my other ear.

"Stop," I whisper, and try to shove his hand away, but his grip tightens on my neck.

"Alice," Katie says checking if I'm still there.

"Oh, um right well my parents are home- and um," I struggle, so overwhelmed.

Ryan takes the phone from me. Fuck!

"Wait!!"

"Hey Katie. Alice is a little busy right now but she'll call you back later." I could practically feel the shock on her face.

I don't hear what she says but Ryan laughs, and moves his fingers so that the tips are inside of me. I whimper and he looks down and smirks, hanging up the phone. His playful manner now gone once again.

"Do you want me to stop?" He grabs my hands and moves them up over my head, his finger now sliding all the way in, my face knotting with pleasure.

"I"- his fingers then move sharply, and he slams against my g-spot. This time I let out a full moan, and he clamps his hand over my mouth.

"Shh. You what?" He says, kissing neck slowly. "I really don't like the way you covered this up." He says brushing my neck.

"Please, -I don't," his fingers stop moving, they stay still inside of me.

"So you want me to stop?" He pushes them a little, and they now rest directly on my gspot. I squirm around but his other hand pushes down on my stomach, and I moan again. "Words."

"I want-" Ugh. "I want you to leave me the fuck alone you piece of shi-!" His fingers pull out, the slam back in, and he cuts off my moan with an aggressive kiss.

I try to pull his fingers out, weakly because it feels so good, but he grabs my wrists, and puts them above my head again. "If you don't keep them there yourself, I'll use other methods." Wha the fucks that supposed to mean. "Mm unless that's what you want?" I huff.

"I'll tie you up b-bitch." I'm out of breath, and trying not to give in but my body is not helping. He looks down at me.

"Do you know what a submissive is?" He pulls his fingers out of me, and I breath a heavy sigh. He didn't even let me finish. I slowly shake my head no.

"Of course not." He rolls his eyes, and sounds annoyed. "Fuck, what am I doing." He drags a thumb along my bottom lip. I attempt to clamp my legs together, for some sort of relief but he's sitting between them.

He gets up off of me, and looks down. My legs are shaking, and he still looks like he's the one who's pissed off.

"I'll see you tomorrow." He says and leaves the room.

7

S omehow he manages to avoid me. He'll come in, no further than my doorframe to wake me up. Then he'll turn up the music in the car so as to not have to talk to me.

It's getting irritating. I mean not that I enjoyed our interactions. But I didn't mind them. At least most of them.

Friday though, there's a party and of course Katie got invited which means I did too. The last party I went to didn't end so well for me, but this time it'll be better.

We get a ride from Jake, we're good now and decided to just be friends. This time I decided to wear a black crop top, and black jeans. It's cold though so I threw on a denim black jacket.

The party was really fun. There were shots in one corner which drew my attention, and a few people smoking in the living room. The house was also huge.

By 12am I'm extremely drunk. Me and Katie are thinking of smoking when a hand slips around my waist. "Hey beautiful," some guy I've never met says to me.

"Heeyyy," I giggle, and spin around to face him.

He's HOT. I want to kiss him. But I also want to smoke. Maybe I'll smoke and kiss him! He's not as hot as Ryan though. God, I hate that man.

Submissive? I should search it up. I sit down on the couch giggling, and someone passes me a joint as I pull out my phone.

I nearly throw it across the room, after I see the images that pop up on my screen. Naked women tied up, being choked, using toys? He wants to tie me up? For real? And what, use toys on me? I only have a vibrator and not a very good one at that. I should tell Katie about it.

"Hey Katie!" I yell before I notice she's right beside me. Someone else heard me too though, and I feel his presence behind me.

"Did you know- I giggle- how good vibrators-"

"Fuck," I hear behind me.

"Ryannnnn! I was gonna come looking for you," I say peering up at him behind me. I'm about to take a hit of the joint but he grabs it, hands it to someone else and grabs my arm aggressively. "Hey! Why are you always such an asshole!"

He drags me up and over the couch, lifting me by my shoulders. "Shut up. Your going home."

"But wait! I need to tell Jaky!" He curses under his breath, mumbling something I can't hear.

Louder he says, "I will drag you into a fucking bedroom and show you who you belong to, if you don't shut up about that guy for one fucking second."

"Oooo someone's jealous," I giggle again, and he stops outside of his car.

He mumbled under his breath but I hear it without the loud music in my ears. He mumbles 'she's drunk' over and over again, taking a deep breath.

He puts me in the car, and buckles my seatbelt. "Waaait!!" I say as we're about to leave.

"What?" He looks over annoyingly.

"Why the hell did you ask me if I knew what a submissive is?? What the hell!!" He swears again under his breath and drives.

His grip is tight on the steering wheel the entire time. I lean my head against the window. "You didn't drink did you? Cuz if you drank that would make you into a baaad driver."

"No. Im sober," he says flatly. He turns a corner sharply.

"Watch itttt," I say and he takes another deep breath.

He pulls into my driveway, and I get out of the car.

He follows me to the front steps, my parents aren't home and I realize I forgot my key. He sighs again and pulls out his extra, opening the door, and closing it behind us.

"You can go home now," I say drowsily.

"Yeah right," he follows me up the steps, and gets to my room before I do, looking for something. "God how can you find anything in this mess?"

I shrug my shoulders and plop onto the bed.

"Where are your pjs?" He asks pissed off, throwing another thing off the floor, into the closet.

"Mmmm, in the drawer I think," then I giggle knowing what else is in there.

He opens it, and pulls out shorts and a tshirt. Then I hear him take a deep breath, look at my innocent smiling face, and turn back around. My vibrators in there.

"Here," he throws the clothes at me and turns to leave.

"Wait, can you unzip my top?" He sighs and comes back. He moves my hair to my shoulder, and trails a hand down my back. He takes the zipper from the top, and I feel his fingers tickle down my back as he undoes the zipper. This top is strapless so it has a zipper to easily get into it.

It drops to the floor, and I turn around in nothing but my jeans, since you can't wear a bra with the top.

Ryans eyes stray down, and his jaw clenches. I pull down my jeans, and shimmy out of them. "I don't want to sleep with pjs on, it's too hot in here," I say quietly.

His eyes come back up to meet mine, and he comes closer, putting a hand in my hip. His hand grabs my chin, and he looks down again. "Can you stay?" I ask.

His breathing is heavy, and I can see the bulge in his black cargo pants.

"Please? I don't wanna be alone." He takes a deep breath, and pushes me back into the bed. Right when I think he's about to leave, he pulls his shirt over his head. He grabs one of the many pillows and blankets from the bed and throws it onto the floor. "Um, you uh don't have to sleep on the floor?"

He looks hard at me, his eyes trailing down my body. He looks like he's about to break. I'm so horny after he left me.

He walks over and gets in the bed, under the covers, but on top of me. His hand wraps around my neck, the other resting beside my head. I gasp. "You. Are really fucking lucky that you're drunk right now." He sighs heavy. My legs squeeze together.

Then he drops to my side, and adjusts the blanket so it's covering both of us. Hes facing me on his side, so I turn to face the wall.

I can't sleep. He's way too close to me, yet not close enough. I scoot myself back, until I feel him against me. I feel him stop breathing, surprised at my closeness.

I'm so horny oh my god. I decide to play with him a little bit. I wiggle my bum to 'get comfortable,' until I feel his dick getting hard again. Then I push back, a bit harder. He grabs my hip, and raises his head to look at me. I look up.

"Stop it," he says.

I shrug. "Stop what?" I see his chest rising and falling, and my eyes roam down on their own. God he looks so good shirtless.

I take my arm, and slowly drag it down, from his shoulder to his v-line. He watches my hand, following the movement all the way down.

"I'm extremely wet right now," I say. He shuts his eyes and says 'fuck' under his breath.

"Alice"-

I take his head and pull it down towards me, kissing him so lightly. I feel it throughout my whole body. "Please," I whisper between kissing him.

"No," he says grabbing my neck again. I feel that straight to my core, thoroughly ruining this pair of underwear.

That's when I decide to grab his dick, and I cup my hand over it. He groans.

"Alice stop." His grip on me falters, but then he squeezes. I choke, and let go. "No. Your drunk."

"But you can tie me up, anything you want I'm just so horny." He shuts his eyes, contemplating.

"Fuck." He grabs my hands, and pulls them over my head. "If you don't keep them there I'll stop. Understood?"

I nod.

"Words, Alice." His tone has changed, and it makes me want to listen to everything he says, but also not listen to see what he'd do to me.

"I'll keep-them th"- I moan as he drags his thumb down, and circles my clit. I arch my back up, but he slams it back down.

"Stay still," he says. He takes my underwear and pulls it down, leaving me fully naked. He sits there for a minute, staring down at me. "You are- so hot."

I smile, catching my breath. He kisses me down my body, leaving hickies everywhere. He kisses down to my thighs, and raises a leg so it's resting on his shoulder. He kisses my inner thigh, and all around where I want him most. My hands are holding on too the headboard, but I push my hips up toward him. "Pleaaase," I whine out.

He pushes them back down. "You take what I give you. I promise you'll finish. Eventually." He says the last part more quietly, and I almost begin to regret asking for this. That when he starts to use his tongue.

"Ohh," I moan and he sucks, and licks my clit. In this raised position, he has easy access. I squeeze my legs around him, and he brings his other hand up, slamming his fingers into me while his mouth is on my clit.

I squirm, and whimper as he hits my gspot easily at this angel. "Stay still," he reminds me. Him bossing me around is so hot.

He hits the spot over and over again, and I get very close to finishing. I grab his head, pulling his hair a little, when he stops. He looks up and pulls his fingers from me. He looks angry.

Fuck. My hands. I throw them back up, frustrated that he stopped right when I was about to finish.

He starts again, and this time it's even more sensitive. He's going really slow, and teasing me once again. I groan, but he just grabs my hips.

I keep my mouth shut, knowing asking him to go faster won't help. He sees I've caught on and picks up his pace. At this point I get to the brink of finishing very fast.

He looks up, and sees my heavy breathing, and my mouth starting to fall open. He slams his fingers into me and says, "if you were sober right now, I'd edge you for hours until you were begging to finish."

I whimper, "please. Don't." He smirks.

I arch my back and cum hard. It was the hardest I'd ever came in my life. I'm shaking, and see stars for a few seconds. He gets up, to go to the bathroom, cleaning his hand and bringing back a towel to clean me.

He gets back into bed, and pulls me close to him. "Darling, your going to be fucking mine."

I smile to myself, and fall into a deep sleep, loving to be held in his arms .

8

My eyes open slowly. I feel so warm. And cozy. To hands are wrapped around me, and I'm laying on something hard. A chest. WAIT. Who's?

My head raises up to see Ryan sleeping, half naked in just his underwear. Oh no no no. I look under the covers and see that I'm practically fully naked. I'm wearing HIS sweater that he wore last night. And nothing else. Fuck.

I get up carefully, trying not to wake him, and successfully make it to the bathroom. I stare at myself in the mirror for a good long second. I can't believe that happened. I practically begged him to touch me. Not only that, but he actually made me finish.

I take a deep breath. It's fine. I'll just go out for a walk and hope he's gone when I get back.

I put my hair up, and grab underwear from my cabinet, and put on the clothes I have laying around on the bathroom floor. I look at my chest and see hickies all over it. Guess no more beach for me next weekend. Great.

I creek the door open into the bathroom, and nearly jump out of my skin when I look up and see shirtless and pantless Ryan, standing in the doorframe. His arms test on either side of the opening, and he's leaning down slightly.

"We're you just going to leave without saying anything?" He asks slowly.

"Um- well, I mean no." I look down to the floor.

He breathes deep, but I breath deeper. Why does he have to be hot. Couldn't he just be ugly. He grabs my chin and lifts it, staring at my slightly bruised neck. And he smirks. Oh god.

"I have to go... um.. walk the cat," I say and push past him. I can walk the 20 minutes to Katie's right? Although she's probably not even home, she has volleyball on Saturday mornings.

I walk about 5 feet away when he grabs my bicep, then the other, and pushes me against the wall. "Sure you are."

Then he leans down and kisses me. And I mean kisses. I kiss him back, and don't try to push away. I wouldn't be able to even if I wanted to.

"Go out with me," he says. More like demands. "Next time you act like you did last night I need to be able to fuck the living shit out of you without feeling like I was taking advantage of you."

I stare up at him. He's the worst. He- he's mean. And the type that would push a freshman into the lockers if they were walking on the wrong side of the hall- ME - type of guy.

He's hot though. And maybe it wouldn't be that bad. But I hate his friends. And him. "No."

He grinds his teeth together. "Why not. Because I'm too old?"

"Welllll, ya. Your going to college in less then a year!"

"I'm living at home though?"

"Oh you are?"

"God you know nothing about me." He sighs, as if just realizing now that this is the most he's ever talked to me.

"As if you know anymore about me. We would never work anyways."

"Why not." He raises an eyebrow.

"My brother wouldn't like it," I say ignoring his question.

"Your brother doesn't like anything to do with you and anyone being together let alone me." He has a point there.

"We'll still no." I say and take a breath to say really fast, "and like, I'm not even attracted to you in that way anyways so"-

"Really...?" His hand comes up from my arm, and itches toward my throat. I watch it, and my breathing speeds up a notch. It comes up and rests at my pulse point, I didn't even realize however that his other hand has moved down to my hip. "Then why's your heart beating so fast?"

I say nothing and grab both his hands pulling them off of me. I walk toward the door, pointing outwards. "Get out."

"You know you were begging me to stay here last night? Remember that? Or how I had you shaking beneath me?"

"I was drunk."

"So your saying"- he takes a step closer- "that if I touched you now you wouldn't be wet? That if I ran my tongue down"-

"Shut up!" Why is he soo... ugh!

"Don't tell me to shut up. And do not interrupt me." He takes his clothes off the floor, and throws them on messily.

He walks over and slams his hand above my head on the wall.

"I'll make you realize you want me. And in the mean time you can stop with the attitude or next time your begging for me to touch you, I won't think twice or hold back everything that I want to do with you."

I gulp and he leaves through the door. That was holding back? What the hell does he want to do to me? Wait.

I look through my google history on my phone. Submissive. The pictures. It wasn't a foggy dream. It was a foggy memory.

I take a screenshot and send it to Ryan, with the caption: another reason.

If he responded, I wouldn't know because I called Jake. I need to get out. Go to the movies. Something.

He picks me up and we decide on smoothies since I already didn't go twice. And man we're they good. He wasn't lying. We laugh and talk, and I tell him a little bit about Ryan. We're actually becoming pretty close friends.

Pretty soon it gets late, but we decide to go to the movies. I check my phone and see three missed calls from Ryan. Whatever. And a bunch of texts like where are you, can we talk, blah blah blah.

He can't just decide to be nice to me all the sudden. Well nice is sugar coating it. More like, harass me just because I let him eat me out. Let him, more like begged him. Ugh.

Jakes phone rings as we're getting popcorn. Apparently there's some sort of family emergency.

So he drops me off at home, and when I walk through the door, Ryan is sitting on my counter eating chips!

"Im going to make your life hell," he says between bites.

"You already do." I slam the door shut, and grab a drink, about to take it upstairs.

"Where were you?" I don't respond.

I have a missed call from Katie so call her before he can say anything else. "Hey!"

"Hey, are you okay? You disappeared last night."

"Oh ya, um I wasn't feeling too good so Ryan gave me a ride home." At the sound of his name, his head pops up and he follows me upstairs. I sit on my bed and he lays down beside me, playing with my stuffed turtle. Since when did he get so comfortable in here?

"OooOo Ryan. Have you fucked him yet??" She says really loudly. So loudly that he hears, and lets out a chuckle, staring at me questionably.

"No! Of course not! I told you I hate him, and he's also sitting beside me right now so I'll talk to you later. Just wanted to let you know Im not dead."

"Awesome, have fun! But not too much"- I hang up the phone and look at Ryan who starts dying of laughter.

"You said that you"-

"Get out! No! Katie is just a horny ass who can't keep her thoughts to herself."

"Mhm. Are you sure?" He grabs my hand and pulls me over, taking my hip and pulling me over his lap so that Im straddling him.

I pretend to be unfazed, but really it's getting annoying. He's so cocky.

He's still holding my hips, and pushes me down so Im sitting directly on him. He's hard. And then my pulse quickens. He moves his hips, and my hands fall on either side of his face, my eyes closing as Im trying not to moan.

"S-stop." One hand comes up behind my head and pulls at my hair, right at the roots. Even beneath me he's still a top. I whimper, and he flips us over so that he's over top of me now.

"If you wanted me to stop, why didn't you get up? Hm?" He pushes his hips into mine, and I let out a quiet moan. He hears it though and smirks. "So Katie's the horny one?"

I get frustrated and try to push him off me.

"Mm nope. Too late. You had your chance," he kisses my neck, trying to leave another hickie.

"No stop! I want to go the the beach tomorrow I already have lots!" I grab his face, trying to push him up.

"Good," he says. Then he brings his hand down.

"Wait, please."

"What? Don't like getting teased? Guess who got to finish last night when the other didn't."

"Is this what this is about?"

"Maybe."

I moan and squirm trying to get out from under him, but he pushes my hands up above my head and circles my clit.

"You should only be aloud to wear skirts. These cargo pants are horrible." Ya right. And give him easy access whenever he wants.

He picks up his pace, and I almost break, asking him to stop teasing and actually do something. "Please. Stop."

He thinks for a minute. "Go on a date with me and I will."

"And if I don't?"

"Then this- he looks down at the pace between us- will become a very regular occurrence."

I breath in deep. A date won't be that bad J guess. And I cannot stand being teased. "Fine."

He smirks and gets off of me. "Skirt on though. And then we're going to the movies."

"Now?"

"Have anything better to do?"

"I have homework."

"Sure you do. Get dressed."

9

- -

Walking into the theatres, I feel like all eyes are on me. He holds my hand the entire time we walk to get popcorn, and only lets go to pay. Then he grabs it again right afterwards. Im not used to it. Physical touch I mean. Especially in public.

We're going to see some action movie. It seems good but not great. And I don't really like the actors in it, but it was his choice and he told me I could pick the next one. As if I would go out with him again.

We sit near the back, and there's barely anyone in here. Probably because the movie sucks.

I start eating the popcorn, and it's probably the only thing that will get me through this movie. And I already start to get cold because of the stupid skirt.

As Im eating the popcorn I slowly start to get a little bit into the movie. And by that, I mean the main actress is pretty cool and she's hot. Wears a leather jacket. But honestly that's the only thing I pay attention to.

I feel Ryan move his hand down to my thigh, and he moves his fingers up and down a bit.

I try to pry his hand away but he leans in and says, "I never said I'd stop at the movies. Just for the moment."

I suck in a breath as his hand moves up my skirt a bit. "Not here!"

"This place is old, cameras are broken it's fine. Friend used to work here." His hand slowly slides further up, and he grabs my chin, "watch the movie." He moves my head to face the screen.

Popcorn forgotten, my eyes stare ahead, even though all they want to do is move down to look at his hand creeping up my skirt. I squeeze my legs together, but he pries them apart.

"If you don't keep them apart yourself, I'll sit you on my lap and hold them wide enough for the whole theatre to see," he whispers. This is so gross, and yet somehow Im so turned on right now. I tell myself its just because he edged me earlier.

I spread them apart a bit slowly, and I can practically sense the smirk on his face. "Please," I try one last time grabbing his arm.

His fingers brush past my most sensitive part, and I know know there's no convincing him.

"If you stay quiet, I might not tease you too much. But you just make it too much fun." I look at him, and he points at the screen. I sigh and look, then nearly jump out of my seat when I feel his fingers quickly move my underwear.

They rest directly on me now, cupping underneath me. My eyes jump around to make sure no one can see us. His hand pushes up against my clit and I look at him as if he were insane while I try to hold in a whimper.

"I said eyes on the screen," he says tauntingly. "Is something wrong?"

"I hate you. Your such a"- his fingers push into me and I moan under my breath, luckily he chose an action movie so there's gunshots hiding my noise.

"I'd watch your mouth. Your not really in a position right now to be testing me. Don't you agree?"

His fingers move deeper, and push against my gspot.

"Answer me."

"I- stop I can't."

"You can. Watch the screen."

I sit back in my chair, and force my self not to move my hips into his hand. "Please." I don't even know what I know asking for at this point.

"Do you want me to stop? Or keep going. Because your mouth is telling me to stop, but your body says otherwise."

"Mm just"- Someone from the front looks behind, and says shhh. He stares for an extra second and Im scared he sees something, but he gives no hints to anything he does and turns back around. "What if-someone sees?"

"Just shut up and watch the movie." Wow. Change in attitude much.

I start to give in to it, and my hips move slightly, and at this new angel my eyes shut, and a moan would've escaped if it weren't for him pulling my chin over to kiss him.

He's a good kisser. His lips are so soft. And he's gentle yet he's in control and he knows it.

It feels so good, and after being teased earlier I can already feel my stomach starting to tighten. I will not cum in front of all these people. I can't!

Im just about to finish, wanting to claw his arm away, even though I know I can't, when he retreats his fingers. "But"- I whine out.

"Bathroom. Now. Go." I follow his order immediately, for whatever reason. Maybe it's my hormones, or maybe it's the tone of his voice. When we get the bathroom, I realize it's an old theatre so the bathrooms aren't stalls.

He pushes me into the bathroom, and moves me so that my arms are pinned against the wall. I try to move them but he keeps them there firmly. He kisses me, and slides his knee between my legs. He kisses me aggressively, practically shoving his tongue down my throat.

Then he moves us to the countertop, and sits me up, this time holding my hands behind my back. If I try moving them he just holds them tighter. "Please I want to"-

"What? Touch me? You touch me and you'll be on your knees in seconds."

I take a breath. Maybe that what I want. But I don't dare tell him that.

He takes his belt off. I feel.. what I get excited? But then he has me stand up, and spins me around.

"Wait, what are you doing?"

He wraps the belt around my wrists and tightens it, keeping them securely together. I try to pull them apart but it stays firmly in place. "Ryan!"

I struggle in his arms, but really I am so turned on by this. "Just let me help you," he says teasingly.

"I don't want your help." He turns me back around, and sits me back on the countertop. My legs are squeezed together, and I've never wanted to masturbate so badly in my life.

He grabs the back of my head, and pulls me toward him, kissing me once more. Even if I wanted to leave and masturbate it's not like I could. He has me tied up and locked in here. Why does that turn me on more though. Ugh.

"Please," I start to ask because Im so horny.

"No," he says simply. He sees me pulling my legs together for relief so of course he pulls them apart and stands between them.

I groan, and try again to wiggle free, but he grabs my hips and pulls my waist into him. Then he grabs my neck, and makes out with me some more. He chokes me whenever I try to move. "P-please" I say panting to catch my breath. I move my hips closer to him and try to move myself against him.

He smirks. "I told you I'd make your life hell." He moves my hips back, his hand wrapping around my thigh. His hand moves up my skirt right where my hips start and his thumb moves to drag around my clit lightly. I groan trying to push in, but his hold on my neck tightens. "Hm, why are you wet right now? I can practically feel it through your underwear." He moves my underwear aside.

Well obviously fucking asshole. His hand finally moves where I want it to, and I nearly orgasm right there when his fingers slide into me. I moan loudly, not even caring if someone hears me.

"Will you finally admit to being mine?" He asks.

"I-Im not," I breath out.

His eyes squint. "Such a brat. I bet you enjoy being tortured like this." My head shakes back and forth quickly. "Fine."

He slows his fingers down to almost a stop. Then he moves my hair out of the way, and begins to leave a hickie on my neck again, making the old one dark once more. I can't even do anything because the longer he stays the faster his finger begins to go.

My stomach starts to tighten, "pleaaase." I beg him.

"No," he whispers softly, and pulls his fingers out of me. I whine out and groan, struggling against him.

"Let me go!!" He chuckles.

"I can. I can even let you finish, with just one simple thing."

I miserably look to the ground. It's getting late maybe he'll take me home and I can just finish myself off. Or I can say I have to pee, to make him leave and do it right here.

He starts to untie my hands, and I sigh. "We're going home. It's late," he says.

" 'We?' " I say.

He lets out a laugh. "Of course. Your not masturbating tonight," he says. "I already have your vibrator. Big mistake showing me where that was." My stomach dips. It's fine I can use my fingers. Not if he's there though!

"You cant sleep over again, my parents will be home tonight," I say smugly.

"Really? Then why is my mom with yours three hours away right now?" Shit. I forgot his mom was visiting with them today.

"Well still, they'll find out. We have cameras you know."

"They don't check those. Otherwise you wouldn't be coming home drunk every other week." I sigh knowing I can't win with him.

We're in the car now, and he opens the door for me. "Well maybe I just don't want you to!"

"Oh love I know you don't want me to. Doesn't change a thing."

10

"Can you at least sleep in the guest bedroom?"

"Nope."

"How about the floor?" He plops down on the bed beside me.

"Nope."

"How about"-

"How about you be quiet, before I make you?" I stare at him blankly. Asshole.

"And how would you do that?" I ask.

He just smirks, pulling his t-shirt and pants off and throwing them in the floor. I stare at him, with no shame knowing he's been doing the same at my sports bra since we got here. Then though he goes under the covers.

"I'm going to the beach tomorrow, you better not keep me up with your snoring."

"I do not snore," he says and pulls me to him.

"Hey! No! You sleep on your side and I'll sleep on mine."

"Again. No." Ugh!! He's impossible.

His one arm is under my head, the other around my waist, my back to his front.

Im so tired of him teasing me and denying me. I turn around in his arms, my hand sliding down his body. I kiss his naked chest lightly, and his eyes shoot open staring down at me. But he doesn't say anything.

So I take my hand and bring it all the way down, finding his dick already hard. I slide my hand into his underwear and grab it, running my thumb over the tip.

He groans and regrettably finally grabs my arm. "If you don't stop"-

"What? You'll put me on my knees? Oo so scary," I say sarcastically, giggling.

He takes a deep breath, and snakes his hand up to my neck. I love getting a rise out of him. "You want to die don't you?"

I shake my head, and try to grab him again. He squeezes my neck though, and pulls my hand away.

"Sleep." He says sternly. He lays back down, and turns me back around.

So teasing him won't work. Maybe I can help myself and tease him at the same time. I take a deep breath. Then my hand slides down my body.

His breathing is steady though, and I think he may have fallen asleep. Maybe that'll be even better. Now I can finally finish.

I start to tease my clit lightly, but I'm so horny I can't stand teasing myself for long. I whimper slightly as I slide two fingers into me, and it feels so good. But his arm around my waist is sort of in the way.

Im very aware of Ryan behind me, but it turns me on more. The thought of him catching me. I moan a little, and soon I forget his presence as pleasure takes over. His fingers are so much better though. Soon I push off his arm, which was difficult, he was squeezing quite tightly.

I moan a bit louder, and start to move my hips into my hand. I don't realize, with my eyes screwed shut, that Ryan woke up. He stares at me, then lightly kisses my shoulder. I almost jump, but instead I groan. "Please touch me," I beg.

He sighs and sits up a bit. "You know I can't let you finish," he warns harshly.

"Please."

One of his hands trails down to my stomach. His other hand grabs my wrist, and pushes my fingers in deep, touching my gspot. I moan out and arch my back upwards.

Then the hand on my stomach pushes it down. I moan loudly, and my eyes roll to the back of my head. It feels so full.

"Please, I'll do whatever you want." Im so desperate. I really don't want him to stop. And I want him to let go of my stomach.

"I told you what I want."

I groan. I try to move my hand out but he keeps it there firmly. I wiggle but it only makes it worse.

"Please," I whine out. Im on the verge of tears now, the pleasure building to be too much.

He shakes his head, and pulls my fingers out, replacing them with his own. He climbs on top of me, and leans down to kiss my lips lightly. "We work. I promise. Just let me show you."

"But"-

"Give in." His fingers slide faster and harder. I moan.

"I- I can't."

"Why?"

I can barley speak now, my breathing fast and short.

"I'll stop."

"Please." Im so close now.

"Tell me what I want."

"God Ryan please."

"Say. It." His fingers slam against my gspot.

"Fine!!" I moan loudly and my body quivers beneath him as I cum hard, pulsing around his fingers. I breath heavy, and see stars.

His hand is still going though. A bit slower but still hard. "Mm stop."

"Fine what Alice?" He smirks. I grab his hand and try to pull it away, but he grabs my wrist and pushes it above my head.

"Ryan!"

"Who do you belong to?" He says still smirking.

"Ugh." He still doesn't stop and I know I can't handle another orgasm. I moan and quietly say, "you."

"Sorry what was that?"

"You you! God. I belong to you" His hand finally pulls out.

He falls beside me, grabbing a towel he hid under the bed earlier. My whole body is shaking as he cleans me up.

He kisses my forehead, and says, "I promise you'll only regret it a little bit." Asshole.

He smiles and I know Ive definitely made a mistake. Maybe.

11

Have you ever wondered what it's like to be completely and utterly in love with the person your in bed with? Me too. And I couldn't tell you. Because I wake up beside the guy that I hate.

I can't control the way my body reacts to him though. He's hot, and controlling, and I hate it. Also very positive that's he's a sadist. I mean he enjoys watching me squirm and tied my hand behind my back in that bathroom!

He's pretty cute sometimes though. It's tough with him. He has such a short fuse. But pissing him off is simply too much fun.

"Goodmorning beautiful," he says in a deep voice. God morning voice is hot.

"What, now that Im 'yours,' your nice to me?" I ask.

"Don't roll your eyes at me." Shit. Did I? See what I mean though, short fuse. But also fun.

"Hey Ryan?"

"Mhm?" This is going to be so funny. Saw it on tik tok.

"Do you ever wonder what it's like to be tall?"

He looks down at me laying on his chest. "Your kidding right? Im 6'3."

"Mmm, well ya your like 6' foot maybe but Im talking about like really tall. You know like 6'5?"

"Are you trying to get a rise out of me right now?" His hand slowly slides up my stomach.

"N-no." My heart rate speeds up and his hand goes around my neck.

"Then why's your heart beating so fast, hm?" My face flushes red. He wasn't supposed to catch on that fast.

"Um, it's hot that's all." He laughs and murmurs sure.

"Your such a brat."

"Why do you keep calling me that!"

He sighs. "Well you enjoy pissing me off right?"

"Of course not," I say sarcastically.

"Why."

"Um"- because then he usually fingers me or chokes me out- "because it's funny?" I say almost unsure.

"Or," he says and flips us over pinning my hands above my head. "You know what I think?" My breathing gets heavy and I feel my arousal dripping between my legs.

"Mhm?"

One hand trails back to grasp my neck and tightens. I whimper a bit. "You like to get put back in your place." I shake my head.

"No! I"-

His hand slides down and I suck in a breath. "Then why are you so wet right now hm?"

I moan as he circles my clit.

He pushes a finger into me and I moan. "Don't worry, I'll fuck all that attitude out of you soon."

I suck in a breath. "No you won't. I"-

"Alice!!! We're home!" My dads calls from downstairs.

"Shit. Get off!" He smirks as I struggle and squirm.

"But watching you squirm- he pushes his fingers into me deep- is just so much fun." I moan and my eyes roll the the back of my head.

"Alice??!" I hear my dad coming up the stairs. I look at him panicked.

He chuckles and rolls off of me.

"Fuck you. Get in the closet you whore." He gives me a warning look, and steps in closing the door behind him. I quickly grab a towel to hide my partially naked body.

"Alice?" My dad steps into the room.

"Oh hey dad sorry I was in the shower," the lie slips out of my mouth as it so often does.

"Oh, no problem."

"I though you guys were coming home later tonight?"

"Oh ya we were, but Ryans mom didn't want him to be alone for too long. Have any clue where he is by the way? His cars there but his mom says he's not."

I shrug. "Not sure, I don't keep tabs on the guy. I can barley tolerate the 15 minute car rides with him. He's probably in the trash can with the rats or something," I giggle. "Seems like his kinda place."

I know I'll prolly get beat for that one.

"Alright, well I'll let you be. Your mum and I are going to step out to get some groceries be back in an hour, K?"

"Sounds good, I'll probably be at the beach with Katie. Later, dad."

He leaves the room closing the door behind him. Ryan steps out of the closet. "Wow! Have you finally come out! I knew you and Kris were dating!!"

"Uh huh. So are you calling your self a rat?"

Welp didn't think of that one. "Whatever. I have to get ready for the beach."

"How you getting there?"

"Katie's mom."

"She's going to drive you two hours down to the beach and two hours back?"

"Well ya I guess."

"I'll drive you. Then I can stay. Katie can invite what's his face if she wants."

"Nope. Nah-uh. You are not inviting yourself to this. We have a ride."

"Well now you have a better one."

"No."

"Yes."

"No."

He walks up to me and looks down. "Yes."

"Why do you want to go so bad."

He squints his eyes at me. "Because I don't want you laying half naked on a beach without me there."

"Possessive much."

"Yeah. And I also would love to see it."

"Fine. Only if you say please," I smile innocently.

"No."

"It's not that hard."

He sighs. "Please, can I come with you?"

"Wow! He has manners!"

"Shut your face or Ill shut it for you."

I giggle and drop the towel. His eyes follow it down. I turn to my closet and pull out a black bikini.

"You are not wearing that."

"Watch me."

As he's standing by the door I shove him out of it and lock it behind him.

"Go get ready!"

I pull out my phone and text Katie to tell her he'll give us a ride and to invite Kris.

15 minutes later Ryans knocking on my bedroom door. "I'm almost ready!"

I quickly shove a towel into my beach bag, and turn to open the door. I put on black jean shorts over my bikini but decide to just buy a shear cover up over the top.

"Fuck."

I smirk and walk past him. My boobs look great in this.

"Change right now."

"Nope we're late let's go."

He takes a breath and chases me down the stairs and out the door. "Front," he calls out.

"Ugh. Kris is coming can't he sit with you at the front?"

His one arm rests on the car, and my back is pushed into it. "Your sitting at the front."

"Your so bossy."

I turn to open the back door, but he keeps it shut, opening the front one.

"Sit your ass down at"-

"The front ya ya."

His jaw clenches. But he lets it go and sits beside me.

"Why is this such a big deal."

"I'm not your uber driver. And plus we're dating J want to sit beside you."

"We are not dating."

"Uh huh."

We pick up Katie and Kris, and they talk between themselves most of the way there. Rock music thrums quietly in the background.

About an hour in, Ryan places his hand on my thigh. I look at it and push it off back onto the gear shift.

Surprisingly he doesn't move it back. I'm in a really good mood today though. I feel like today is going to be my turn to tease him.

12

"**S**top." Ryan grabs my hand and pushes it away from him.

Teasing him is sooo much fun. He's rock hard in the middle of the beach, and he's extremely pissed off. I reach for him again, and he grabs my wrist, pulling my face right up to his.

"If you don't stop right now, I will rail you right in the middle of this beach without hesitation," he whisper yells to me. I smirk.

"Please?"

Kris and Katie are in the ocean, swimming and splashing, and jumping over the waves.

He grits his teeth, and looks out to them. "You better hope your enjoying yourself now because you won't be when we get home."

I squeeze my legs together in anticipation. He's so hot when he's angry. But a small part of me wants to piss him off even more. Get a rise out of him.

Maybe Im just horny.

"Well it's not my fault your such a horny teenager. One touch from me and your practically quivering."

He looks at me and his facial expression is filled with angry but also lust. He looks down at my half naked body. Then he thinks over what I said. Then he probably thought about all the teasing I've done.

"Your trying to piss me off," he accuses.

"Pshhh. What??? No!" I shake my head.

"No? Really?" He shifts over on the towel to lean into me. "If we were alone, I'd be punishing you right now. But that what you want isn't it?"

"N-no."

"Maybe I'd edge you till I see a tear fall down your face. Or I'd make you cum so many times, you'd loose track of it. I'd tie you up to my bed so your completely helpless and mine to do with as I please."

My eyes squeeze shut trying to shut out his words. "Shut up."

His hand wraps around my thigh. Then one goes almost around my neck. "Are you going to stop?"

"Mmm no," I say looking him in the eyes.

His eyes look like they light up a bit. He wants to punish me. You can see it. He wants me to be tied up, and he wants to see me cry.

"You know, maybe I just want to enjoy a nice day at the beach without your horny ass trying stuff all the time."

"Oh I'm sorry, who was the one who can't keep her hands to herself today?"

"I hate you."

He laughs.

"Shut up."

"No you don't love. Come on let's go get ice cream from that stand over there. You've been eyeing it almost as much as me.

I blush. I blush. Ew! But still I'm excited. They have all the good flavours.

He gets chocolate (basic bitch), and I get cotten candy. "Your such a child," he says to me.

"Your just jealous cuz you chose an ass flavour."

"You don't like chocolate?"

"Well I like chocolate but nothing that's like chocolate flavoured I guess."

"Weirdo."

"It's gross! Kinda tastes like dark chocolate."

"Not really," he says looking down at his cone.

I take mine up to my mouth and flick my tongue all the way around it, then from bottom to top.

"Don't do that." I didn't even notice him staring at me.

"Hey! Guys!" Katie comes running over to us, almost tripping over her own feet.

"What's up oh my gosh slow down."

She turns to Ryan, "can you drive us home?"

"Why? I thought you guys wanted to stay for sunset?"

"Oh shoot. Right."

"What's the rush," I ask her.

"Oh um well," she blushes and looks towards the ground. Oh so she's horny.

Ryan smiles and looks towards Kris, coming out of the water now. He looks down at his watch then towards the sky. "Well sunset is in an hour, so do we want to wait for that and then take off?

"Yeah sure," Katie smiles.

"Sounds good to me," I say in agreement.

When it comes, Katie is kissing Kris, and I take a quick photo of them (they'll thank me later). It's a really nice photo.

Ryan pulls me so Im sitting in front of him, and we look out at the ocean. "I love it here, I wish it weren't so far," as Im saying this, him hand sneaks forward to wrap around my stomach.

"Why not get a car so you could come more often?"

"I don't want to get a job to pay for it," I say smiling.

"Fair enough, lazy ass."

"Hey!"

He chuckles.

I turn around to face him, my hand falling between us. It brushes against him when it falls.

"Watch it," he says and lifts it to place it beside us.

"And if I don't?" My other hand comes between, and I grip him, covered by our legs.

He groans. "You are so fucking dead tonight."

"My parents are home tonight."

"We'll then I guess you'll just have to stay quiet," he smirks and pulls my hand away, pinning both to the sand on either side of us.

"No, your not coming tonight."

"More like your not coming tonight," he smirks and I blush. "My moms out of town, you'll stay at my house.

"But"-

"Say your staying at Katie's."

"Yeah right. Im not doing that or going anywhere with you."

"Mhm except your mine so you don't get to decide that. Unless I have to convince you?"

"Impossible. How would you do that?"

"Well. You'll just have to find out."

We leave the beach, and get into the car packing everything up. Kris and Katie cannot get their hands off of each other. Disgusting.

Ryan places his hand on my lap again, but this time when I move it off, he places it right back then tightly squeezes when I try to remove it again.

"Ryan stop," I whisper as he slowly moves it down between my thighs.

It's dark in the car, and Katie and Kris are busy talking and kissing.

"Ryan," I jump up when his hand skims my clit.

"Say you'll sleep over and I'll stop."

"No!"

I grasp his arm, and gasp as it pushes against me. I nearly whimper, and noting this he pulls away to turn up the music.

Immediately his hand returns, and rubs faster.

"Okay! Fine! Jeez." I whimper.

He smirks and quickly looks over. "Are you alright? You seem flustered."

"Shut up."

The rest of the ride home is fine. We drop them both off at Kris's house, and I shoot my mom a text saying that I'll be staying over at Katie's. I bet she did the same with me.

We pull into Ryans driveway, quickly running into the house so my parents don't see.

When we walk up to his room, his mood changes slightly. "Shower," he says. "Let's go."

"Um ya no."

He raises an eyebrow at me. "No? You're going to go to bed with sand all over you?"

"No, as in no Im showering with you."

"Why not? Saves water."

"I'd rather not."

"As if you have a choice."

He pulls me to the shower, and I struggle to get away. He stops and wraps his hand around me neck, backing me into his bathroom.

"If you want to shower by yourself, fine. But it'll only make your punishment that much worse."

I squint my eyes at him. Then I close the door in his face. Screw him and his punishments. I quickly shower, and realize I don't have underwear or pjs.

"Ryan!"

"Yeah?" It sounds almost as if he were expecting it.

"Um, can I borrow some pjs?"

"Mhm. Open the door."

I open the door a sliver, and shove my hand through holding my towel to my body. He opens the door more, and pushes him self through.

"Hey!"

His eyes wander down my body, and he steps closer, walking behind me.

My breathing falters, as his body is pressed against mine, his hand snaking up my front. "W-what are you doing."

"Drop the towel," he says into my neck. His other hand fists a dark red tshirt.

"No." I sound shaky. And his hand that was going up now wraps around my throat.

"Drop. It." He squeezes tighter.

One of my hands grips his forearm. "N-no."

"Do you want the tshirt? I'll only give it to you if you let me put it on."

I roll my eyes, and reluctantly drop the towel to the floor. I can feel him staring at my tits, as he pulls the shirt over my head.

Then his hand falls back to my neck, and the other goes to my core. I take a sharp intake of breath.

"Hm what's wrong?"

He rubs slow hard circles and I moan a little, gripping onto his arm to help stay up.

Then his finger pushes into me and I gasp as it hits my gspot. "S-stop," I moan.

He pulls away, and picks me up throwing me over his shoulder. I notice that he's already showered. "When did you"-

"I used my moms."

"Put me down!"

He throws me onto the bed. "Hands up."

"No!"

He takes a deep breath, "don't make me repeat myself tonight."

I pull my hands up, my heart racing, and he lays down onto of me. He grips my chin, one hand beside my head and kisses me harshly.

I take my hands, and knot them in his hair. He groans, and stops kissing me. "You need a safe word."

"A what?"

"In a few seconds I will not hold back, so give me a word and only if you say that word will I stop."

"Um-uh peach?"

He nods his head, and slams my hands to the bed. He pulls my shirt up with one hand, and takes my nipple into his mouth. My back arches up towards him, and I whimper as he sucks it harshly.

After he moves on to the next one, he sits up and says, "stay there for a moment."

I nod and watch him as he moves to his drawers and comes back holding something.

"Give me your wrists."

My eyes widen and I start to shake my head. "No! You are not tying me up!" I sit up and move back.

He grabs my ankles and pulls me back down. Then he quickly wraps his hand around my neck, and I whimper helplessly as he stares down.

"No?" He laughs. "It's not like you could stop me."

Then he's grabbing my wrists and in a few seconds they're hand-cuffed to the bed frame. "Please.."

"Save the begging for later. You'll need it."

13

Handcuffed to the bed, theres little I can do but to accept Ryans hands as they pry my legs apart. He starts to tease me lightly, and soon I'm so wet I can practically feel it dripping.

"Mm, looks like someone's enjoying herself," he says to me and I blush.

He gets up, and I can't see what he's grabbing out of his nightstand drawer. Then I hear buzzing. My heart stops in my throat.

"Miss this?" He pushes my vibrator into me, and the c shaped toy circles around to attack my clit. I squirm, and having not had it for so long my body reacts to the feeling almost immediately and I moan loudly.

He turns up the speed and I shut my eyes, tilting my head upwards. "W-wait."

"Eyes on me," he says lowly.

I shake my head. He moves up and starts to kiss my neck. Then hes sucking and is likely leaving a massive hickie.

"Stop!"

"Then keep your eyes on me." I look down and make eye contact with him. I'm practically panting now, and try not to whimper as he pushes the vibrator onto me harder.

"Tell me when you're close." I look down his naked torso, and see the bulge in his pants.

"L-let me help you," I say struggling, trying to get free. I want to touch him, help him for once.

"You want to?" His eyes look at me with so much lust and power.

"P-please."

He pushes against my clit, and kisses me. "You just want to be let free," he whispers. Damn it.

"Nooo.."

"Nice try. But don't worry. You'll help me." My stomach starts to tighten, and my mouth falls open a bit. "I mean if you want to so badly."

My back arches, and right as I'm on the brink of ecstasy, he pulls my vibrator away from me.

"Nooo, please."

"Keep begging." He says, throwing the vibrator away on the bed. He replaces the vibrator with his fingers.

"Mmm I don't beg." His fingers slow. Then something changes his mind, and he speeds up, and pushes hard. He finds my g-spot and attacks it.

He slides his fingers out to the very tips, and then slams back in against it. I moan out, and take deep breaths, the hand cuffs pulling my hands back hard.

"Slow d-down." After all the teasing I already feel myself getting close.

"No." I arch my back upwards, and turn my head to the pillow, feeling my core contracting. I cum hard, feeling myself squeezing his fingers uncontrollably. I whine out and, squirm under him, his two fingers pushing my gspot, and staying there.

I shake my head back and forth, "s-stop! Please." I'm extremely sensitive, and I feel everything at almost double. "Stop!"

"Beg. Me," his fingers slam into me, his thumb moving to my clit. Then his fingers push onto my gspot once more, and his other hand comes to push my stomach down.

I buck under him, trying to get away. His hand on my stomach, pushes it down to the bed, successfully holding me still. The added pressure makes me feel so full, his hands brushing against every wall inside of me. "P-please," I try.

"Please what?" He says almost mockingly.

"Please, stop," I whimper out.

"Say sir." He says wrapping a hand around my neck, knowing exactly how to make me feel helpless.

"No!" I look at him, but then he grabs the vibrator.

"No?" He turns it on.

"Wait! Please"- My voice breaks.

"Just say it." Asshole. He is not doing this. I'm not submissive!! There's not a chance in the world that I'll be calling him anything but a bitch

"No! Asshole Im not sub"-

I practically scream when he pushes the vibe hard on my clit.

"PLEASE."

"Say it."

"No!" I cry out. I shove my face into the pillow, my body trying to get away from him.

"Then no." He moves up to me, and his hand tightens on my neck. I suck in a breath. Why does choking turn me on so much.

"Please," I say looking at him in the eyes. Now though, I'm not sure if I'm asking him to stop or keep going.

"You know I won't until you say what I want."

"Fuck. Ryan, please." I try to squeeze my legs together but that only makes it worse.

"Just say it."

I pant hard. If I finish I'll probably black out. "Pleease.." I try one last time.

He just looks at me. Then I start to feel my stomach contracting.

"...bitch," I whisper, squirming and moaning out.

"God just fucking say it you brat."

"Mmm, fuck but"- I cry out again, when he pushes the vibrator hard into me, the inside shoving up against my walls.

I don't know how much more I could handle. And I know I could use the safe word but... maybe I am submissive. This is really hot. Not being in control, but knowing I still safe.

"Please... please sir," I whisper out quietly.

"Sorry what was that," the pressure on my neck lightens, and he pulls the vibrator away a bit.

"Please sir, I'm sorry."

"For what," he says knowingly.

"Just- please." He finally takes the vibrator away, and removes his hand off my neck. His hands move to either side of my head and he kisses me lightly but dominantly.

"For what." He says still wanting an answer.

I blush red and quickly say, "for teasing you today and not listening."

His eyes squint. He kisses me one more time, then his hands go up to my wrists and he quickly releases them from the cuffs.But when they're realized he still holds them down.

"On your knees. Side of the bed."

He gets up off me and I squint at him, hesitating. But then he raises and eyebrow and slides a hand up my middle thigh, and I scramble to get to the floor. No way is he doing that again. He smirks.

"Good girl."

I sigh angrily. When I'm on my knees, I look up at him sitting on the edge.

"Have you done this before?"

I shake my head yes. "Once ya, a while ago... I don't really remember much of it though."

"Later, tell me about it later."

He rips his belt of, and slide his pants down his legs. Now fully naked before me, he's even hotter then ever. Holy shit.

He grabs the back of my head, gripping my hair to guide me down, but then lets go to see what I'll do.

I grab him with one hand, look him in the eyes, and lick him bottom to top. "Fuck," he says.

Then I circle the tip with my tongue and push it down to the back of my throat. He groans, and grabs my head again, but doesn't force anything.

I decide to tease him a little, and slowly move up and down. I flick the tip once I reach the top with my tongue, then go back down.

My hands grip his thighs, and I come back up and down going very slow. "Alice..." He says in warning.

"Mmm?"

He groans. "Don't do that."

I giggle internally. Then I speed up a bit, but a few seconds later I slow back down.

"Fine have it your way." His grip on my head tightens. "Two taps for peaches," he grits out.

Then he slams himself into my throat. I nearly choke but hold it in, just whimper a little. He continues this a few times, and god it's hot.

"Use your tongue more," he says. I love advice, it's helpful and makes me feel better to know Im doing what it is that they like.

I push my tongue along the bottom, and he groans once more.

After a few minutes he he lets go of my head, and cum goes down my throat. I swallow instinctively, but know that he let go of me incase I didn't want to. He's so sweet, but would kill me if I said that out loud.

He pants, and says fuck again under his breath. He pulls me up to him, me still in his shirt, and kisses me. Then he moves to my neck and kisses me more. He slides his hands up my torso and pulls the shirt over my head, taking a nipple in his mouth.

I moan as he flicks it with his tongue, "please. No more." I whine. He flips me onto my back.

"And who would stop me," he says smiling. "You know for someone who 'isn't submissive' you sure seemed to enjoy that a lot. If I checked, would you be dripping again?"

My legs try to close instinctively, but he's sitting between them. "I'll tie you up one day, you know," I say angrily.

"You can try," he says smuggly.

He rolls down beside me, and pulls me into him, throwing the light covers over us.

"Why do you just keep handcuffs in your room?"

Against his chest, I look up, but he just smiles. "Incase I had to kidnap you to get you in here."

I roll my eyes at him, and of course now he looks down. His hand quickly goes around my throat again, "did I not punish you enough already?"

"Sorry," I squeak out. He smirks.

"Sorry what?"

"Nope," I say and grab his hand pulling it away from my neck.

"You will call my sir in bed." He says

"Not a chance. That was the last time."

"Well see," he says and pulls me in even closer tohim, and I pass out not 10 minutes later.

14

- -

I wake up beside him for the second day in a row . And for the third time in general. Every time I've woken up naked. This man...

This man will be the death of me. I roll out of bed, and drag myself to the bathroom. I realize that I don't even have a tooth brush. Or a hair brush. Or clean underwear to wear home. I guess it's just a minute to. Get there. I can wear none, and just steal some sweat pants.

I go over to his closet, and walk in. It's a full walk-in and it's almost completely black. Jeez. This is cheery. I at least have some reds and purples. I find some sweatpants and shove my legs into them. I also put the t-shirt back on that somehow got thrown in here. I turn to leave, but Ryan's standing at the doorway, his hands resting on either side of the frame.

"Did you ask if you could borrow those?" I try to keep my eyes on his face, but with him naked and standing like that, my eyes can't help but wander down. It's as if he knows this and smirks.

"I did actually, you were sleeping." I shove around him, grabbing my stuff and getting ready to leave. It takes ample amounts of effort not to turn around.

"Where are you going?"

"Home? I need to brush my teeth with my tooth brush and eat and get clean underwear."

"I have all those things."

"Ew, Im not using your tooth brush that's disgusting."

He rolls his eyes, and goes to his bathroom searching through the cabinets. He pulls out a brand new tooth brush, still in the packaging. "Clean enough for you, princess?"

I snatch it and shut the door behind me.

"You know for someone who just got punished, you're acting oddly bratty. Do you need a repeat of yesterday?"

I lean myself against the counter top. "Shut up!" I yell through the door.

He laughs, and I hear his retreating footsteps.

When I come back out he's also in sweatpants, but with nothing else. Why is that so hot?

"I'll make pancakes if you say please sir again," he says with a smirk.

"You wish. I'll take the pancakes though."

"Mmmk but it will cost you."

"And what would his majesty want?"

"Stop sassing. Maybe I just want something fun. Like I make you pancakes but you have to make me a smoothie."

"Uh huh but it's not that is it."

"Well no," he smirks. " I was thinking more on the lines of something like..." He pretends to look deep in thought, "you going on another date with me?"

I squint my eyes at him. "Where."

"It's a surprise," he shrugs.

I sigh, "fine. But these better be some darn good pancakes."

He grins and pulls me in to kiss me on the cheek. "Promise."

He jumps his way down the stairs and throws himself into making them.

"What do you like on them?" He asks me once he's almost done. Something about men in kitchens- ugh.

"Um- my gaze is pulled down to his shirtless torso, and the way he flips them, his hands mixing-

"Alice."

My head snaps up, "hm? With jam. Strawberry if you have it."

His eyebrows scrunch together. "Not maple syrup? Weirdo. What kinda Canadian are you."

My lips curl up into a smile as he hands me my plate of pancakes with lots of strawberry jam slathered onto it.

"Thank you."

He hums and sits down beside me. "Tomorrow I have a game. Come watch it?"

"Is this the date?"

"No."

"Then no."

"What kinda date would that be??"

I shrug, my mouth filled with pancakes, "one where I didn't have to talk to you," I shove my face with more.

"Jesus, your going to choke calm down."

"These are really good. I haven't had pancakes in forever."

"Yeah I could imagine."

I clean up for the both of us since he cooked, and grab some milk out of the fridge.

"Do you want to sleep over again tonight? We can go to school together tomorrow. My mom just texted, said she'll stay with my grandparents another day."

"Wow! Your asking me this time??" I say sarcastically.

"Well we have school, I wasn't sure if your parents would let you."

"They're gone again they won't care."

He gives me a sidelong glance. Almost pity, but not really. He sighs, and looks back to his food. He has like 6 pancakes on his plate, jesus.

"So you'll stay?" He asks hopefully.

"Aw, are you lonely."

He gets up and wraps his arms around me from behind. "Maybe Im just horny," he says.

"Mhm."

Im still so tired, I barley slept last night since we stayed up for so long. We watch tv together for some time, but I think I fall asleep shortly after, because I wake up in his bed beside him.

Perfect.

15

This man needs to get taught a fucking lesson. Im not a fucking sub. And now he's helplessly asleep beside me. I get up and head to the drawer that sits in the dresser on the far side of the bedroom. He doesn't stir. I guess he didn't get enough sleep either.

When I open it my jaw drops. It's an organized drawer of little sections containing dildos, vibrators, handcuffs, buttplugs, you name it. Jesus christ. What did I get myself into. I knew he had some stuff, but this??

I pull out some handcuffs. These ones are red, and look like they'll hurt if you pull on them too much. Good. The attached key goes onto the top of the dresser, far out of his reach. Or mine I suppose, but he'll be staying there for a while.

I turn to him, mischievously smiling, as I take his wrists and cuff them to the bed frame. I also gently pull his pants and boxers off. Then I lower myself to his neck, and start to leave a hickie. About ten seconds in he jolts awake.

"Alice," he groans as I palm his dick. His neck moves to give me more access. Then he realizes where his hands are, as he tries to grab my waist.

"Mmm?" I say still leaving a now very dark hickie.

"Alice," he says this time with warning coating his voice. "What the fuck do you think you're doing." He tries to shake me off him.

His wrists snap upwards- he swears under his breath from the metal-, and his hips buck upwards, "stay still, or you won't finish," I whisper giggling.

He breathes heavy. Then his legs come up on either side of me, and wrap around my arms and chest. They push my back down towards the bed and Im trapped under them.

"Hey!!"

"Where are the keys?!" He shouts angrily at me.

"Im not telling you! Just listen to me, do what I tell you, and I'll let you go afterwards."

He practically growls. "No you listen to me. If you want to live to see another day, you will uncuff me right fucking now."

I try to wiggle free, but he holds me down. "Let me go."

"Are you going to free my hands?"

"Yes... eventually."

He breathes deeply. "Fuck. Your going to regret this, I hope it's worth it for you."

He slowly releases his legs. Hell ya.

I jump up an wrap my hand around him, pumping slowly. He takes a breath and tries to buck up into my hand, always craving control. I place my hand on his hip and gently place it back down. "Take what I give you," I taunt, repeating his own words.

"Alice I swear to"- he groans as my thumb circles the the tip.

"What was that?"

He clenches his jaw and stays quiet. I admire the way his shoulders look, hooked up like that, and he scowls at me. "Don't get used to it. After this, you'll never want to see me again."

A shiver goes down my spine. He's like, really mad. I giggle. Maybe I am a brat.

I turn my head back down to his chest, and suck to leave another hickie. His hips buck up again, and so I remove my hand from him, and place it on the bed frame over his head, staring down at him in the eyes. A gentle smile plays on my lips.

"If you don't behave like a good boy, I'll have to stop," I say quietly.

"You're pushing it darling," he says through gritted teeth.

"Remember that until Im pleased, you're stuck here."

He doesn't say anything and clenches his jaw.

"What do you say?"

He squints his eyes at me.

"Yes ma'am." I say in answer. My hand moves down to his dick when he says nothing. I grab his balls and squeeze, he winces. "What, do you say?"

If looks could kill, he'd probably have blown my head off. "Yes. Ma'am." He says slowly, death staring me. I smile.

I remove my hand and kiss down his chest. Then I lick him all the way up his dick, making eye contact with him as I do so. He groans, and almost bucks me off of him.

I can barley believe I'm actually pulling this off. I bring him to the very edge, and when I feel him tense up I stop. "Alice, I swear to fuck, if your only trying to piss me off there were other ways to do it. Congratulations, you've earned your punishment now fucking let me go."

"Aw, but I wouldn't wanna let you go before you've finished."

"Oh believe me"- he grunts as I slide a thumb over the tip- "I'll fucking finish."

I smile innocently at him. I may be pushing him a bit too far. Oh well. "You're going to have to stop swearing at me, unless you want me to gag you."

His eyebrow lifts up. He stays quiet but his eye twitches. My mouth goes back down and he finally stays still. His groans are the only sounds coming out of him.

My hand slips down to my already wet core, and I pause to get my pants and underwear off. Then I sit up and slip my fingers inside of me. Ryan watches with lustful eyes. His gaze turns me on more and I slip him back into my mouth.

When I feel him getting close again, I slow down and my hand replaces it. He gives me a glare. "Are you not going to ask permission to cum?" I challenge, panting now, from my finger.

His breathings heavy, his body now desperate for a release. He's still rock hard. My stomach twists at the sight of him, legs clenching together.

"A simple please will do," I whisper. My hand pulls away from myself.

He stays quiet. So I continue sucking him, and then stop once more at the last minute. "Fuck, Alice"-

"Mmmm what did I say about swearing?"

His teeth grit.

"You can't say please if your mouth is gagged. Then how will you finish? You're practically shaking already."

He stares hard at me and twitches when my thumb brushes over the tip again. "Alice.."

"Don't you dare try to tell me what to do." His mouth shuts. "Tell you what. I'll give you a use for that mouth then once Im satisfied, I'll help you too okay?"

He groans as my hand squeezes hard up to the top.

"What do you say?"

"Yes..."-I don't let go- "ma'am."

I smile lovingly. Then I crawl up the bed and turn around. "You better be quick unless"- I moan out as he raises his head and sucks hard on my clit. "Good boy," I say mockingly. He bites my clit slightly and I jump up whimpering.

I grab his balls and squeeze. He groans. "Stop. Unless you want to be edged again I highly recommend you do it properly," I whisper.

"Sit back down." He says through a clenched jaw.

I lower myself once more.

"More." He says, and I do. He sucks my clit, and half of me wants to uncuff him so that he can use his fingers as well. His tongue slips inside of me, already very wet from all this. I moan out, and he picks up his pace.

I hold on to his chest, barely keeping myself up. This is a lot harder then I thought. After already playing with myself I was already almost on edge, and all this has turned me on so much. Not the actual tying him up, but the anger that came with it.

I almost scream out, at the thought of what he'll do to me after, I cum hard. I scramble off of him, not wanting him to keep going. After yesterday I'm already sensitive.

"Thank me," I pant out.

"For what?!" He almost yells out. He pulls against the restraints, clearly having enough. "You've had your fun. Let. Me. Out!" He yells at me.

"But Im not done with you yet," I smile. My confidence is wavering though. He's really mad. I have a hand down his chest.

Suddenly there's a knock on the door. "Hey, I've got your jersey, I let myself in, are you in there?" I'm not sure who it is, but obviously someone from his team. Shit. Ryans head slowly turns to me.

"Last chance. To let me go." He says lowly and scarily calm.

I get up, put my pants on and walk to the door. It's fine I'll just answer it. The bed isn't visible from the door. I open it, and I think his names Camden. He's close friends with Ryan, the two have known each other for as long as I can remember. "Hey, Ryans not home, but I'll take it," I smile up at him.

Only problem is my legs are shaking. And why would I be alone in his bedroom. He squints his eyes at me. "Where is he?"

"I meant he's in the bathroom," I say quickly. "Ya he's taking a shower. Just um wait downstairs and"-

He pushes past me and into the room. His eyes perk up in amusement. "Dam. And here I though we were doms."

Wait. We? He looks down at me.

"How the hell did you get him to"-

"Cam grab the fucking key."

"Ohh I see." He chuckles. Then he turns to me. "Where is it?" He says.

"Um-" His tall lean frame towers over me, maybe even as much as Ryans. I feel so small. He's also almost as intimidating as Ryan is. I look over to him, and he's staring daggers in my direction. I turn and run.

Not a chance I'm going to be alone in a room with these two. But before I run three steps, Camden wraps an arm around my waist and easily pulls me to him. He leans down, his mouth to my ear.

"As much as this was probably really hot to watch you top, I'm going to need the key sweetheart."

My breathings fast. I look toward the dresser, but then quickly avert my gaze to the nightstand hoping he didn't catch that. He did.

He smiles devishly. Ryan looks close to exploding for some reason, now more so then before.

"So tell me, how did you ever manage to do this hm?" He throws me onto the bed, and before I can scramble off, Ryan wraps his legs around me.

I don't say anything, and he walks over with the key. "I- Im sorry," I look at Ryan, pure fear in my eyes.

"Oh you will be." Camden unlocks one wrist, then the next, as I desperately try to wiggle free. But as Ryan gets up to stretch his shoulders, Camden climbs on top of me and moves my wrists above my head. Ryan throws him handcuffs and a long bar. Fuck. Me.

- -

16

R yans practically has smoke coming out of his ears. I think that's why he's letting Camden be the one to tie me up. Ryan looks through drawers, now a weirdly steady expression on his face. It's stern but not angry. Scary.

Camden on the other hand, seems serious but a bit playful. I can tell that finds this whole thing funny.

And then there's me. I'm shitting balls right now. I have no idea what he'll do.

Ryan turns to me, and speaks for the first time in a while. "Do you remember your safe word?" He asks. He stands by the dresser, stark naked and still rock hard. Camden seems unfazed and even took his shirt off.

"Yeah. Um peaches. Sir."

"Good girl." Camden says to me. "Did Ryan get a safe word?"

"No. I figure he could've used mine. But I mean maybe he was enjoying himself"- Ryan wraps a hand around my neck and I loose my voice before the next words come out.

"I highly suggest you shut the fuck up right now."

"What do you say?" Camden asks a small smile playing on his lips as he looks down at my naked body. I realize now that he isn't staying here to be intimidating. He's here to embarrass me.

Camdens arm moves to cup my breast, and he squeezes my nipple. In my already aroused state by the two of them staring down at me, my core tightens, and arousal drips down my thigh.

"Yes- yes"-

"Yes- Yes. Yes what?" Camden says raising an eyebrow mocking me.

"Yes sir," I barley get out when Ryan releases his grip a little. "Please- I'm sorry."

"Aw Cam look who's apologizing now?" Ryan looks to him and smiles. My hands are tied up above my head and I've never felt more helpless "Spread your legs." He says demandingly.

Camden moves to my side and starts to suck on my nipple while Ryans watches. "N-no." I say. Not a chance.

"Fine if you don't want to, I'll use the bar."

He lifts the black metal bar off the bed. It has two cuffs on each end. I shake my head and shut me legs tighter, squirming under Camden trying to get away. But he takes a hand and wraps it around my bust, keeping me securely still. Once my nipple practically hurts from how hard it's gotten he moves on to the next and I whine out. But I stay still.

Ryan grabs my leg and attaches it to the bar. When he tries to put the other one on though, the fight returns and I bring it up to kick and squirm. "Pleaseee no." I say. He grabs my leg and pins it down to the bed, looking up at me.

"Maybe you should've thought about this before"-

"I said Im sorry!"

"Mmm darling, I know." He clamps my legs into it, my legs now being forced apart. I blush at the exposure, arousal drips down onto the bed.

Camden moves a hand down my thigh. My core aches to be touched, practically pulsing. Ryan moves a thumb to my clit and I close my eyes and moan. "Open your eyes and look at him," Camden says. I shake my head. He grabs my throat and squeezes. "I may think what you did was funny, but don't think Im on your side," he whispers into my ear. Then his hand slips down, and he pushes into me right to my gspot finding it immediately. I whimper, both their hands down there making me squirm.

"Whatever." I say closing my eyes and turning my head away.

Cam pulls my face by my throat to face him. "Look at me. And say that again."

My stomach flips with knots. His finger slams against my gspot and holds it there. The bed dips beside me and Ryan leaves once more. "I said whatever." I shouldn't be pushing him. Not if he's anything like Ryan.

His teeth grit. He laughs. "Fuck Ryan she's brave." He slams his fingers in and out of me, and I hold back embarrassing whimpers.

"Please. Stop." I breath heavily.

Ryan comes back holding 3 items. He holds out a metal sphere looking thing. "Ever used one of these before?"

I shake my head and Camden laughs.

"Sucks." he says. He passes it to Camden and in one go he shoves it into me, my arousal allowing it to slide in. Moaning, I arch my back upwards. But just as he begins to slide it in and out, he removes it. I whine, but not a moment later I feel him probing at my back entrance. My face pales.

My arousal works as lube, and it pushes into me. "This okay?" Cam asks. Ryan doesn't seem to care. He's handling the next thing. I give him a tiny nod.

My face bunches up at the weird feeling, hurting just a little. I feel so weirdly full. I can't imagine something being in both entrances at the same time.

My body squirms. "Stay still like a good girl Alice," Cam mocks. "Do you not like that?"

I feel my cheeks pink as he stares down, and I stay still. Why does he have to be here for this.

I hear a faint buzzing in the background. My heart jumps to my throat. My head shoots to Ryan, but Cam grabs my face and pulls me to kiss him. Shocked, I try to move away but then I feel the vibrator hit my clit.

I moan into Camdens mouth, as it slides inside of me. "Keep kissing him. If you stop, I'll stop." I moan again and kiss him very messily.

Already finishing earlier, I now feel over stimulated and am close to finishing within 2 minutes. I rock my hips against the toy. Camden stops, and kisses my shoulder.

Ryan moves the toy away. "Whyy," I whine out.

"I told you if you stop, I stop."

"But!"-

"Shut up." He turns the vibrator on its highest setting and pushes it on my clit again. I jump, and shove my head into the pillow. "Please- I said sorry"- my own moan cuts me off. My nipples almost hurt now as Camden goes back down to them.

Ryan moves up to my face. "Sorry what?"

"Sorry sir!"

"Beg me." His finger move and he shoves them all the way in, in one go. Im so wet, it drips onto the bed.

Cam gets up and moves to the dresser bringing back two clamps. "I think she needs some more motivation."

Ryan smirks. My face flushes. "Please. Can I finish?"

"Please what?" He says slamming his fingers into my gspot.

"Sir!! Please," my legs are shaking, and I feel my stomach contracting.

"Mmm let me think." Camden clamps one nipple and I whimper. Fuck that hurts. But also feels good. "No." He pulls his fingers and the vibrator away, and Camden puts the other clamp on.

"Ughh." I pull at the restraints a little.

"Aw are you horny. Weird that your so wet, I though you said you were such a 'dom.' Doesn't seem like it."

His degrading words only turn me on more. "Shut up."

"Don't tell me to shut up." He pulls one of the clamps up, and I make a strangled noise.

Ryan watches this, then puts the vibrator back. I scream, and finish, my whole body shaking. "Fuck. I'm sorry"-

"Cam"-

"Yeah ya," he gets off the bed and leaves the room. I can hear his zipper undoing, probably going to jerk off in the guest room.

"I"-

Suddenly he slams into me. I scream again, still recovering from my high. I then moan and it starts to feel so good. "Eyes open."

I open my eyes, and he grabs my throat. I moan into his mouth as he kisses me.

"You are not aloud to finish. This is for my pleasure. Not yours."

"But"- my stomach starts to contract, and my eyes roll back. "Please."

He slams into me hard, over and over. He's now panting and squeezes my neck harder.

I'm barley holding back now, and when I feel him finishing inside me, I cum. Hard. Harder than I ever had before. He won't stop.

His hand replaces his dick and he thrusts hard. I might pass out. "Please- stop Rya-sir." I moan arching my back.

"Say sorry."

"I did!"

"Again."

"Sorry sir," I cry out.

He smirks. "Have I officially broken the brat?"

A tear falls down my face, and he finally stops.

"Open your eyes." I open them to look at him, not even thinking. "So submissive." He kisses my cheek and unties me.

17

"D o you not want to finish darling?" he says as he unties me.

His hand goes to my clit, and pushes. I practically jump and grab his arm trying to pull him away. Though through all of this, I knew if I said my safe word it would all be over. But... I liked it. I didn't want it to be.

"Move your fucking hand Alice." My hand slowly moves to the side, and squeezes the bedsheets. He smirks. I shake my head and nearly punch him. But of course I don't.

"Please not again." I whimper as a finger slides inside of me.

"But your still so wet. You look so pretty like this, submitting to me with my cum dripping out of you."

I moan as he thrusts into me. "Please."

"Please what? Please stop? Keep going? Harder?" He smirks as he pushes his finger into my gspot. I moan, and he kisses me.

I feel as though I may pass out, but I also have never been better. He pulls his fingers out, and kisses my cheek.

"If you ever pull something off like that again, I'll do far worse understand me?" I nod my head fast. He kisses down my body, and takes a thigh over his leg. He kisses my inner thigh, and I pull at his hair lightly to try and get him away.

"I said okay! Please!"

"I didn't say we were done. Tell me love, how fast would you finish if I ate you out right now? Would you be able to hold back?"

My ragged breathing fills the room, and I screw my eyes shut, knowing I'll let him do whatever he wants. And he knows it too. My leg falls open wider as he pulls my hips toward him.

Camden walks clumsily through the door and takes in the scene before him. "Ryan, man she's going to pass out, let her be." He stares at me intensity but doesn't make a move forward.

"Can. Get out."

"But- well I really think"-

Ryan sighs, cutting him off. Then looks to me, but the anger is gone. He looks me up and down. "Safe word. Why didn't you use it."

"Um"- my face flushes red.

He slowly smirks. "Unless your enjoying this? You wouldn't mind me making you pass out."

It wasn't a question and I don't dare answer.

"Fucking hell," Camden says and leaves the room. "Find me another one!" He yells back once in the hallway.

I blush hard and giggle. Ryan takes a breath and lays down beside me, pulling me into him. "Rest. I'll go make us some food."

"Sooo.... I'm forgiven?"

He chuckles and leaves the room. Fuuuck.

It was still worth it though.

....

I wake up two hours later, feeling awake and happy. Turning to the door, throwing on some boxers and a tshirt on the way, I stumble my way down the stairs. I'm starving.

I hear quiet chatter when I get there, turning to see Camden and Ryan gulping down kraft dinner.

"Did you leave any for me?" I ask genuinely curious.

"Of course, I made two boxes."

"Ah."

I turn around and reach up to grab a plate, I hear a slap in the background.

"Hey!" Camden says.

"Stop it," Ryan warns.

When I turn around Camdens smirking. "It's not like I haven't seen more."

My face flushes. He looks at Camden. "That was a one time thing. I was angry. Am angry," he says staring me down at that last part. My legs clench as I sit down beside them. Ryans left hand falls down to my thigh in a possessive way.

"Was," I whisper.

His hand slides up my bare thigh, and that shuts me up. He shovels more food into his mouth. Subject closed.

"You know I would just love do that again some time. She is very entertaining. Maybe next time I'll leave uou tied up a bit longer though."

"And you- Ryan points his fork at him- are about to have this fork stabbed through your dick."

Camden hold up both hands, "hey hey hey.. I mean you had no problem sharing earlier I thought maybe"-

Ryan cuts me a glare and clenches his jaw.

"Not even drunk?"

"Only if she admits she liked it." He smirks still making direct eye contract.

My face flushes a deep red and I look down at my food, moving the macaroni around. "I- I don't. Didn't I mean."

"Uh-huh. Then why are your legs squeezing together so tightly, hm? Are you thinking about when"-

"Shut up. They are not."

"I think that's a win for me," Camden says smiling.

"Yeah. Drunk though."

"Not a problem. This ones drunk every other day," he says pointing at himself.

"All drunk." He says.

"Or when in need of desperate help." Cam says laughing a bit. Ryans hand closes in a fist.

"So Alice. Your friend- Kate... what's her name?"

"Katie. What about her?"

"She taken?"

"Um ya she's talking to someone. Also, I don't think she's um... really your type." His eyes squint.

"What's that supposed to mean."

"Well um, your very like intimidating. But like you like to um..."

"She's not a sub?"

My head shakes no. He sighs. "Just clone her will you?" He says looking at Ryan.

"Psh ya right. You couldn't handle a little devil like her. Softie. What would you have done today? Given her a talk?"

"I still think you should've just let her top you, that was some hot fucking shit. Instead you came close to knocking her out."

Ryan smirks. Oh lord save me from these two.

18

I walk over to Ryans house one night with my sketchbook in hand. His moms out tonight, so I'm sleeping over. I drew up the plans for his room. It's a old city skyline, with overgrown plants and cars in the middle of streets. It doesn't have too much detail yet, but I'm hoping he'll like it.

"I thought I said 7," he says when he hears the door closing behind me. It's 7:30.

"I'm only 30 minutes late," I say to him dripping down my stuff. Which is just school stuff since he bought me a tooth brush and lets me wear his clothes.

"30 minutes is a long time."

"Not really." I say walking over.

He kisses my cheek and looks down at the sketch book. "That for my wall?"

"Yeah, you like it?" I say hopefully.

"Love it," he says.

I smile and blush. "It's going to have more detail once I put it on the wall and"-

He cuts me off with a kiss, grabbing my neck and pushing me towards the hallway. Against the wall, a knee slides between my legs and I moan as his thigh moves against my bare clit.

"Good girl," he says. He told me to come in a skirt with nothing under it.

"Can we play a game?" I say.

"Depends on the game." He says squinting at me suspiciously.

"It's fun I swear." I grab his hand and pull him up to his room. I go to the drawer with the toys but he slams it closed.

"Explain this 'game.'" I sigh.

"Just let me into it."

"After what happened last time?"

I smirk. And he scowls. "Okay fine. It's like hide and seek. You go hide somewhere in the house and I have 20 minutes to find you. Whatever time I have left over I get to do whatever I want with you for that remainder of time. And your not aloud to stop me."

"Right. Very funny."

"It'll be fun!!"

He sighs and whispers "how am I supposed to say no to your cute little face." He takes my face in his hand and kisses me. "Fine. But I'm adding a rule. Pick a good enough hiding spot and it'll go into my time. If you can't find me after 20 minutes, however much longer it takes you I get to do stuff to you for that time."

I think hard. It won't take me more than 10 minutes to find him. I'm good at this game. But why would he agree. He's a big guy, there's not that many places he could hide. "Deal."

He smirks. "Count to 60."

"And you have to stay in the house."

"You never said that," he says smiling.

"Ryan!!"

"Fine, fine. In the house."

I inhale, and count as fast as I can already at 10 before he starts running away.

When I hit 60 seconds, I open my eyes and decide to head upstairs first.

His house isn't huge, it's not as big as mine but also bigger than your average family home. I check under every bed and in every closet quickly and decide he's not upstairs. I check my watch, 15 minutes left.

I run downstairs and check in the living room, dinning room, and kitchen. Even in the pantry cabinets, but he's not in there. 11 minutes left.

I look next in the basement, down in the movie room and laundry but again he's not there. Well shit. Why did I say only 20 minutes. I have 8 minutes left.

I check the backyard thinking maybe he'd trick me into saying that's part of the house, but he's not there. I do another round of checking upstairs. It's now been 35 minutes since he went to hide. I'm close to just giving up.

I get a text on my phone from Ryan. It says:

'Here's a hint: Check ceilings.'

What?? What is he? Spider-man? Ugh.

It takes me 10 minutes of checking the ceiling in ever room and closet, when I find a latch in his in the closet on the ceiling. When I open it a ladder can be pulled down. I slowly creep up the ladder and when I get up, there's a tiny attic area, filled with blankets and pulls. The ceiling is black, and there's a small window on the left hand side. It's big enough to crawl, not to stand.

On either side of the window there are also little bookshelves lined with books. "Ryan?"

"You found me," he says from behind and crashes down with me onto the floor. He lands on top of me and kisses my face.

"This place is so cute."

"Yeah, I love it in here. My dad built it when I was young."

I smile. He checks his watch. "Hm look at that, 30 minutes over." My face turns red.

"That isn't fair, I didn't know about this room."

"That's too bad," he says and pins my arms above me. "It's okay. 30 minutes isn't that long, remember?"

I groan.

His hand slides down my body. "Hm what can I do to you for 30 minutes. Maybe I should tease you. Could you wait 30 minutes to cum while I'm pounding into you?"

I squirm under him, regretting coming up with this game. "How about you get 20 minutes. That's how long I had to find you."

"Mmm nope. Those weren't the rules. Lay down my little toy."

As I'm laying down, he strips me of my clothes until Im in naked in front of him. He's still fully clothed.

He runs a hand down my body, and slowly circle my clit only to find Im already soaked.

"Hey" Ryan says grabbing my face," eyes on me gorgeous." Jesus christ.

When my eyes meet his he rams a finger inside of me, and I quickly grab at his arm.

"Oh, looks like my rag doll wants an extra 5 minutes." My hand drops down and I stay still.

"No, please." His fingers go deep inside, finding my gspot. He pushes against it again and again. I moan and work hard not to arch my back upwards.

"Rag dolls don't make noise Alice." I grunt and shut my eyes as he moves faster.

My hands grip the blanket beneath me. "Timer. You didn't set a timer," I say.

He smirks and grabs his phone out. He sets sit for 39 minutes. "Hey! It's been like 5 already."

"You moved remember?"

Grabbing my arms, he spins me over so that I'm laying on my stomach. Then he takes off his belt and ties them together.

"Just in case you try to move again." He reassures.

He kisses my back, and grabs my hips to pull them up. My face pushes into the blankets, and my knees dig into the floor.

A hand runs over my ass. He moves my hair out of my face, tucking it behind my ear then pauses. "You have a tattoo?" He asks surprised.

"Yeah got it when I turned 16." The tattoo is a fairy wing, coming out from behind my ear.

"It's cute." He says then rams inside of me, gripping my hair by the roots. I moan out loudly, his other hand circling around to rub my clit.

"Not s-so hard," I breath heavily.

"Aw too bad you don't get to choose." Out of spite he rams in harder, and deeper.

I almost scream when he hits one spot. "Please!!"

My hands grip the blankets under my head. He picks up my arms and puts them back down to remind me not to move. "You can do it, only 25 minutes left."

"Only?" I moan. I suppress an orgasm I feel coming, just as I feel him spilling inside of me.

He pulls out before I can finish. He flips me over, and circles my clit slowly torturing my body.

I want so badly to push my hips against his hand. He then uses his mouth, and I moan out feeling his warm tongue slowly moving and sucking. His fingers reach up and push into me, and he pushes downs spot on my stomach.

I'm so desperate I shake. He never gives enough, and I can only feel the constant build up. "Please." I whine.

"Brats don't get to finish."

"I didn't do anything!!"

"If only I have a shit." He smirks. I've had enough and grab his arm pulling it away. He slams it down by my head. "You still have 10 more minutes left."

"I don't care!!" I use my hands again to quickly slide inside of me and I moan.

He watches me for a minute, and as Im close he then grabs my hands and forcibly slows my finger down. Than pushes my fingers all the way in, and holds my hand still. A tear slides down my face. "Pleease," I beg.

"No," he whispers and the timer goes off. He shuts it off. "Go down and get on the bed."

Hoping he'll actually do something I hurry down the the ladder.

CPSIA information can be obtained
at www.ICGtesting.com
Printed in the USA
LVHW020403111122
732651LV00010B/918